Karen Morrison and Lucille Dunne

Cambridge IGCSE®

Mathematics

Core Practice Book

CAMBRIDGE
UNIVERSITY PRESS

CAMBRIDGE UNIVERSITY PRESS
Cambridge, New York, Melbourne, Madrid, Cape Town,
Singapore, São Paulo, Delhi, Mexico City

Cambridge University Press
The Edinburgh Building, Cambridge CB2 8RU, UK

www.cambridge.org
Information on this title: www.cambridge.org/9781107609884

First published 2012

Printed and bound in the United Kingdom by the MPG Books Group

A catalogue record for this publication is available from the British Library

ISBN-13 978-1-107-60988 - 4 Paperback

Cover image: Seamus Ditmeyer/Alamy

Cambridge University Press has no responsibility for the persistence or
accuracy of URLs for external or third-party internet websites referred to in
this publication, and does not guarantee that any content on such websites is,
or will remain, accurate or appropriate. Information regarding prices, travel
timetables and other factual information given in this work are correct at
the time of first printing but Cambridge University Press does not guarantee
the accuracy of such information thereafter.

IGCSE® is the registered trademark of University of Cambridge International Examinations.

Contents

Example practice papers can be found online, visit education.cambridge.org/corepracticebook

Introduction

This highly illustrated practice book has been written by experienced teachers to help students revise the *Cambridge IGCSE Mathematics* (0580) Core syllabus. Packed full of exercises, the only narrative consists of helpful bulleted lists of key reminders and useful hints in the margins for students needing more support.

There is plenty of practice offered via 'drill' exercises throughout each chapter. These consist of progressive and repetitive questions that allow the student to practise methods applicable to each subtopic. At the end of each chapter there are 'Mixed exercises' that bring together all the subtopics of a chapter in such a way that students have to decide for themselves what methods to use. The answers to *all* of these questions are supplied at the back of the book. This encourages students to assess their progress as they go along, choosing to do more or less practice as required.

The book has been written with a clear progression from start to finish, with some later chapters requiring knowledge learned in earlier chapters. There are useful signposts throughout that link the content of the chapters, allowing the individual to follow their own course through the book: where the content in one chapter might require knowledge from a previous chapter, a comment is included in a 'Rewind' box; and where content will be practised in more detail later on, a comment is included in a 'Fast forward' box. Examples of both are included below:

◀ REWIND

You learned how to plot lines from equations in chapter 10. ◀

FAST FORWARD ▶

You will learn much more about sets in chapter 9. For now, just think of a set as a list of numbers or other items that are often placed inside curly brackets. ▶

Other helpful guides in the margin of the book are as follows:

Hints: these are general comments to remind students of important or key information that is useful when tackling an exercise, or simply useful to know. They often provide extra information or support in potentially tricky topics.

Tip: these are tips that relate to good practice in examinations, and also just generally in mathematics! They cover common pitfalls based on the **authors'** experiences of their students, and give students things to be wary of or to remember in order to score marks in the exam.

The *Core Practice Book* mirrors the chapters and subtopics of the *Cambridge IGCSE Mathematics Core and Extended Coursebook* written by Karen Morrison and Nick Hamshaw (9781107606272). **However**, this book has been written such that it can be used **without the coursebook**; it can be used as a revision tool by any student regardless of what coursebook they are using.

Also in the *Cambridge IGCSE Mathematics* series:
Cambridge IGCSE Mathematics Core and Extended Coursebook (9781107606272).
Cambridge IGCSE Mathematics Extended Practice Book (9781107672727)
Cambridge IGCSE Mathematics Teacher's Resource CD-ROM (9781107627529)

Remember 'coefficient' is the *number* in the term.

! Tip
It is essential that you remember to work out *both* unknowns. Every pair of simultaneous linear equations will have a pair of solutions.

Reviewing number concepts

1.1 Different types of numbers

- Real numbers can be divided into rational and irrational numbers. You will deal with rational numbers in this chapter. Irrational numbers are covered in chapter 9.
- Rational numbers can be written as fractions in the form of $\frac{a}{b}$ where a and b are integers and $b \neq 0$.

  (Integers are negative and positive whole numbers, and zero.)
- Integers, fractions and terminating decimals are all rational numbers.

> **Tip**
>
> Make sure you know what the following sets of numbers are: natural numbers, integers, odd and even numbers and prime numbers.

Exercise 1.1

1 Copy and complete this table by writing a definition and giving an example of each type of number.

Mathematical name	Definition	Example
Natural numbers		
Integers		
Prime numbers		
Square numbers		
Fraction		
Decimal		

2 Include numbers to show what each of the following symbols means. For example $100 > 99$.

(a) $>$ (b) $\leq$ (c) $\approx$ (d) $\therefore$

(e) $\sqrt{}$ (f) $\neq$ (g) $\geq$ (h) $<$

3 Look at this set of numbers.

$$3, -2, 0, 1, 9, 15, 4, 5, -7, 10, 32, -32, 21, 23, 25, 27, 29, \frac{1}{2}$$

(a) Which of these numbers are NOT natural numbers?

(b) Which of these numbers are NOT integers?

(c) Which of these numbers are prime numbers?

(d) Which of these numbers are square numbers?

4 List:

(a) four square numbers greater than 100.

(b) four rational numbers smaller than $\frac{1}{3}$.

(c) two prime numbers that are > 80.

(d) the prime numbers < 10.

1.2 Multiples and factors

- A multiple of a number is the product obtained when multiplying that number and an integer. The lowest common multiple (LCM) of two or more numbers is the lowest number that is a multiple of both (or all) of the numbers.
- A factor of a number is any number that will divide into the number exactly.
- The highest common factor (HCF) of two or more numbers is the highest number that is a factor of all the given numbers.

To find the LCM of a set of numbers, you can list the multiples of each number until you find the first multiple that is in the lists for all of the numbers in the set.

FAST FORWARD

You will use LCM again when you work with fractions to find the lowest common denominator of two or more fractions. See chapter 5. ▶

You need to work out whether to use LCM or HCF to find the answers. Problems involving LCM usually include repeating events. Problems involving HCF usually involve splitting things into smaller pieces or arranging things in equal groups or rows.

Exercise 1.2 A

1 Find the LCM of the given numbers.

   (a) 9 and 18   **(b)** 12 and 18   **(c)** 15 and 18   **(d)** 24 and 12

   (e) 36 and 9   **(f)** 4, 12, and 8   **(g)** 3, 9 and 24   **(h)** 12, 16 and 32

2 Find the HCF of the given numbers.

   (a) 12 and 18   **(b)** 18 and 36   **(c)** 27 and 90   **(d)** 12 and 15

   (e) 20 and 30   **(f)** 19 and 45   **(g)** 60 and 72   **(h)** 250 and 900

Exercise 1.2 B

1 Amira has two rolls of cotton fabric. One roll has 72 metres on it and the other has 90 metres on it. She wants to cut the fabric to make as many equal length pieces as possible of the longest possible length. How long should each piece be?

2 In a shopping mall promotion every 30th shopper gets a $10 voucher and every 120th shopper gets a free meal. How many shoppers must enter the mall before one receives a voucher and a free meal?

3 Amanda has 40 pieces of fruit and 100 sweets to share amongst the students in her class. She is able to give each student an equal number of pieces of fruit and an equal number of sweets. What is the largest possible number of students in her class?

4 Sam has sheets of green and yellow plastic that he wants to use to make a square chequerboard pattern on a coffee table top. Each sheet measures 210 cm by 154 cm. The squares are to be the maximum size possible. What will be the length of the side of each square and how many will he be able to cut from each sheet?

1.3 Prime numbers

- Prime numbers only have two factors: 1 and the number itself.
- Prime factors are factors of a number that are also prime numbers.
- You can write any number as a product of prime factors. But remember the number 1 itself is *not* a prime number so you cannot use it to write a number as the product of its prime factors.
- You can use the product of prime factors to find the HCF or LCM of two or more numbers.

Exercise 1.3

You can use a tree diagram or division to find the prime factors of a composite whole number.

1 Identify the prime numbers in each set.

    (a) 1, 2, 3, 4, 5, 6, 7, 8, 9, 10

    (b) 50, 51, 52, 53, 54, 55, 56, 57, 58, 59, 60

    (c) 95, 96, 97, 98, 99, 100, 101, 102, 103, 104, 105

2 Express the following numbers as a product of their prime factors.

    (a) 36   (b) 65   (c) 64   (d) 84

    (e) 80   (f) 1000   (g) 1270   (h) 1963

3 Find the LCM and the HCF of the following numbers by means of prime factors.

    (a) 27 and 14   (b) 85 and 15   (c) 96 and 27   (d) 53 and 16

    (e) 674 and 72   (f) 234 and 66   (g) 550 and 128   (h) 315 and 275

1.4 Powers and roots

- A number is squared (n^2) when it is multiplied by itself ($n \times n$).
- The square root ($\sqrt{n}$) of a number is the number that is multiplied by itself to get the number.
- A number is cubed (n^3) when it is multiplied by itself and then multiplied by itself again ($n \times n \times n$).
- The cube root ($\sqrt[3]{n}$) of a number is the number that is multiplied by itself twice to get the number.

FAST FORWARD

Powers greater than 3 are dealt with in chapter 2. See topic 2.5 indices.

Exercise 1.4

1 Calculate.

    (a) 3^2 (b) 18^2 (c) 21^2 (d) 25^2

    (e) 6^3 (f) 15^3 (g) 18^3 (h) 35^3

2 Find these roots.

If you don't have a calculator, you can use the product of prime factors to find the square root or cube root of a number.

    (a) $\sqrt{121}$ (b) $\sqrt[3]{512}$ (c) $\sqrt{441}$

    (d) $\sqrt[3]{1331}$ (e) $\sqrt[3]{46656}$ (f) $\sqrt{2601}$

    (g) $\sqrt{3136}$ (h) $\sqrt{729}$

3 Find all the square and cube numbers between 100 and 300.

4 Which of the following are square numbers and which are cube numbers?

1, 24, 49, 64, 256, 676, 625, 128

5 Simplify.

    (a) $\sqrt{9} + \sqrt{16}$ (b) $\sqrt{9 + 16}$ (c) $\sqrt{64} + \sqrt{36}$

    (d) $\sqrt{64 + 36}$ (e) $\sqrt{\dfrac{36}{4}}$ (f) $\left(\sqrt{25}\right)^2$

    (g) $\dfrac{\sqrt{9}}{\sqrt{16}}$ (h) $\sqrt{169 - 144}$ (i) $\sqrt[3]{27} - \sqrt[3]{1}$

    (j) $\sqrt{100 \div 4}$ (k) $\sqrt{1} + \sqrt{\dfrac{9}{16}}$ (l) $\sqrt{16} \times \sqrt[3]{27}$

1.5 Working with directed numbers

- Integers are directed whole numbers.
- Negative integers are written with a minus (−) sign. Positive integers may be written with a plus (+) sign, but usually they are not.
- In real life, negative numbers are used to represent temperatures below zero; movements downwards or left; depths; distances below sea level; bank withdrawals and overdrawn amounts, and many more things.

Draw a number line to help you.

Exercise 1.5

1 If the temperature is 4 °C in the evening and it drops 7 °C overnight, what will the temperature be in the morning?

2 Which is colder in each pair of temperatures?

    (a) 0 °C or −2 °C   **(b)** 9 °C or −9 °C   **(c)** −4 °C or −12 °C

3 An office block has three basement levels (level −1, −2 and −3), a ground floor and 15 floors above the ground floor (1 to 15). Where will the lift be in the following situations?

    (a) Starts on ground and goes down one floor then up five?
    (b) Starts on level −3 and goes up 10 floors?
    (c) Starts on floor 12 and goes down 13 floors?
    (d) Starts on floor 15 and goes down 17 floors?
    (e) Starts on level −2, goes up seven floors and then down eight?

1.6 Order of operations

- When there is more than one operation to be done in a calculation you must work out the parts in brackets first. Then do any division or multiplication (from left to right) before adding and subtracting (from left to right).
- The word 'of' means × and a fraction line means divide.
- Long fraction lines and square or cube root signs act like brackets, indicating parts of the calculation that have to be done first.

Remember the order of operations using BODMAS:

Brackets
Of
Divide
Multiply
Add
Subtract

FAST FORWARD

The next section will remind you of the rules for rounding numbers. ▶

Exercise 1.6

1 Calculate and give your answer correct to two decimal places.

    (a) $8 + 3 \times 6$ **(b)** $(8 + 3) \times 6$ **(c)** $8 \times 3 - 4 \div 5$

    (d) $12.64 + 2.32 \times 1.3$ **(e)** $6.5 \times 1.3 - 5.06$ **(f)** $(6.7 \div 8) + 1.6$

    (g) $1.453 + \dfrac{7.6}{3.2}$ **(h)** $\dfrac{5.34 + 3.315}{4.03}$ **(i)** $\dfrac{6.54}{2.3} - 1.08$

    (j) $\dfrac{5.27}{1.4 \times 1.35}$ **(k)** $\dfrac{11.5}{2.9 - 1.43}$ **(l)** $\dfrac{0.23 \times 4.26}{1.32 + 3.43}$

    (m) $8.9 - \dfrac{8.9}{10.4}$ **(n)** $\dfrac{12.6}{8.3} - \dfrac{1.98}{4.62}$ **(o)** $12.9 - 2.03^2$

    (p) $(9.4 - 2.67)^3$ **(q)** $12.02^2 - 7.05^2$ **(r)** $\left(\dfrac{16.8}{9.3} - 1.01\right)^2$

(s) $\dfrac{4.07^2}{8.2-4.09}$ (t) $6.8+\dfrac{1.4}{6.9}-\dfrac{1.2}{9.3}$ (u) $4.3+\left(1.2+\dfrac{1.6}{5}\right)^2$

(v) $\dfrac{6.1}{2.8}+\left(\dfrac{2.1}{1.6}\right)^2$ (w) $6.4-(1.2^2+1.9^2)^2$ (x) $\left(4.8-\dfrac{1}{9.6}\right)\times 4.3$

1.7 Rounding numbers

- You may be asked to round numbers to a given number of decimal places or to a given number of significant figures.
- To round to a decimal place:
  - look at the value of the digit to the right of the place you are rounding to
  - if this value is ≥ 5 then you round up (add 1 to the digit you are rounding to)
  - if this value is ≤ 4 then leave the digit you are rounding to as it is.
- To round to a significant figure:
  - the first non-zero digit (before or after the decimal place in a number) is the first significant figure
  - find the correct digit and then round off from that digit using the rules above.

Exercise 1.7

FAST FORWARD

Rounding is very useful when you have to estimate an answer. You will deal with this in more detail in chapter 5. ▶

1 Round these numbers to:

  (i) two decimal places
  (ii) one decimal place
  (iii) the nearest whole number.

  (a) 5.6543   (b) 9.8774   (c) 12.8706
  (d) 0.0098   (e) 10.099   (f) 45.439
  (g) 13.999   (h) 26.001

2 Round each of these numbers to three significant figures.

  (a) 53 217   (b) 712 984   (c) 17.364   (d) 0.007279

3 Round the following numbers to two significant figures.

  (a) 35.8   (b) 5.234   (c) 12 345   (d) 0.00875
  (e) 432 128   (f) 120.09   (g) 0.00456   (h) 10.002

Mixed exercise

1 List the integers in the following set of numbers.

$\frac{3}{4}$ 24   0.65   −12 $3\frac{1}{2}$ 0   −15   0.66   −17

2 List the first five multiples of 15.

3 Find the lowest common multiple of 12 and 15.

4 Write each number as a product of its prime factors.

(a) 196   **(b)** 1845   **(c)** 8820

5 Find the HCF of 28 and 42.

6 Simplify:

(a) $\sqrt{100} \div \sqrt{4}$ **(b)** $\sqrt{100 \div 4}$ **(c)** $\left(\sqrt[3]{64}\right)^3$ **(d)** $4^3 + 9^2$

7 Calculate. Give your answer correct to two decimal places.

(a) $\dfrac{5.4 \times 12.2}{4.1}$ **(b)** $\dfrac{12.2^2}{3.9^2}$ **(c)** $\dfrac{12.65}{2.04} + 1.7 \times 4.3$

(d) $\dfrac{3.8 \times 12.6}{4.35}$ **(e)** $\dfrac{2.8 \times 4.2^2}{3.3^2 \times 6.2^2}$ **(f)** $2.5 - \left(3.1 + \dfrac{0.5}{5}\right)^2 (3.3)^2$

8 Round each number to three significant figures.

(a) 1235.6   **(b)** 0.76513   **(c)** 0.0237548   **(d)** 31.4596

Tip

Most modern scientific calculators apply the rules for order of operations automatically. But if there are brackets, fractions or roots in your calculation you need to enter these correctly on the calculator. When there is more than one term in the denominator, the calculator will divide by the first term only unless you enter brackets.

Making sense of algebra

2.1 Using letters to represent unknown values

- Letters in algebra are called variables because they can have many different values (the value varies). Any letter can be used as a variable, but x and y are used most often.
- A number on its own is called a constant.
- A term is a group of numbers and/or variables combined by the operations multiplying and/or dividing only.
- An algebraic expression links terms by using the + and – operation signs. An expression does not have an equals sign (unlike an equation). An expression could have just one term.

Exercise 2.1

> **Tip**
>
> An expression in terms of x means that the variable letter used in the expression is x.

1 Write expressions, in terms of x, to represent:

    (a) a number times seven

    (b) the sum of a number and twelve

    (c) five times a number minus two

    (d) the difference between a third of a number and twice the number.

2 A boy is p years old.

    (a) How old will the boy be in five years' time?

    (b) How old was the boy four years ago?

    (c) His father is four times the boy's age. How old is the father?

3 Three people win a prize of $\$x$.

    (a) If they share the prize equally, how much will each of them receive?

    (b) If the prize is divided so that the first person gets half as much money as the second person and the third person gets three times as much as the second person, how much will each receive?

2.2 Substitution

- Substitution involves replacing variables with given numbers to work out the value of an expression. For example, you may be told to evaluate $5x$ when $x = -2$. To do this you work out $5 \times (-2) = -10$

Exercise 2.2

REWIND

Remember that the BODMAS rules always apply in these calculations.

1 Evaluate the following expressions if $x = 5$.

(a) $4x$ (b) $12x$ (c) $3x - 4$ (d) x^2

(e) $-2x^2$ (f) $14 - x$ (g) $x^3 - 10x$ (h) $x^3 - x^2$

(i) $3(x - 2)$ (j) $\dfrac{6x}{2}$ (k) $\dfrac{4x}{10}$ (l) $\dfrac{80}{x}$

(m) $\dfrac{12x}{4}$ (n) $\dfrac{2x - 4}{2}$ (o) $\sqrt{9x^2}$ (p) $\dfrac{3x^3}{2x^2}$

Take special care when substituting negative numbers. If you replace x with -3 in the expression $4x$, you will obtain $4 \times -3 = -12$, but in the expression $-4x$, you will obtain $-4 \times -3 = 12$.

2 Given that $a = 2$, $b = 5$ and $c = -1$, evaluate:

(a) abc (b) $2bc$ (c) $\dfrac{b^2 + c}{a}$ (d) $4ac - 3b$

(e) $6c - 2ab$ (f) $2(ab - 4c)$ (g) $(abc)^3$ (h) $2(a^2b)^3$

3 The formula for finding the area (A) of a triangle is $A = \dfrac{1}{2}bh$, where b is the length of the base and h is the perpendicular height of the triangle.

Find the area of a triangle if:

(a) the base is 12 cm and the height is 9 cm

(b) the base is 2.5 m and the height is 1.5 m

(c) the base is 21 cm and the height is half as long as the base

(d) the height is 2 cm and the base is the cube of the height.

2.3 Simplifying expressions

- To simplify an expression you add or subtract like terms.
- Like terms are those that have exactly the same variables (including powers of variables).
- You can also multiply and divide to simplify expressions. Both like and unlike terms can be multiplied or divided.

Exercise 2.3

Remember, like terms must have exactly the same variables with exactly the same indices. So $3x$ and $2x$ are like terms but $3x^2$ and $2x$ are not like terms.

1 Simplify the following expressions.

(a) $5m + 6n - 3m$ (b) $5x + 4 + x - 2$ (c) $a^2 + 4a + 2a - 5$ (d) $y^2 - 4y - y - 2$

(e) $3x^2 + 6x - 8x + 3$ (f) $x^2y + 3x^2y - 2yx$ (g) $2ab - 4ac + 3ba$

(h) $x^2 + 2x - 4 + 3x^2 - y + 3x - 1$

Remember, multiplication can be done in any order so, although it is better to put variable letters in a term in alphabetical order, $ab = ba$. So, $3ab + 2ba$ can be simplified to $5ab$.

Remember,
$x \times x = x^2$
$y \times y \times y = y^3$
$x \div x = 1$

2 Simplify.

(a) $4x \times 3y$ **(b)** $4a \times 2b$ **(c)** $x \times x$ **(d)** $3 \times -2x$

(e) $-6m \times 5n$ **(f)** $3xy \times 2x$ **(g)** $-2xy \times -3y^2$ **(h)** $-2xy \times 2x^2$

(i) $12ab \div 3a$ **(j)** $12x \div 48xy$ **(k)** $\dfrac{33abc}{11ca}$ **(l)** $\dfrac{45mn}{20n}$

(m) $\dfrac{80xy^2}{12x^2 y}$ **(n)** $\dfrac{-36x^3}{-12xy}$ **(o)** $\dfrac{y}{x} \times \dfrac{2y}{x}$ **(p)** $\dfrac{xy}{2} \times \dfrac{y}{x}$

(q) $5a \times \dfrac{3a}{4}$ **(r)** $7 \times \dfrac{-2y}{5}$ **(s)** $\dfrac{x}{4} \times \dfrac{2}{3y}$ **(t)** $\dfrac{3x}{5} \times \dfrac{9x}{2}$

2.4 Working with brackets

- You can remove brackets from an expression by multiplying everything inside the brackets by the value (or values) in front of the bracket.
- Removing brackets is also called expanding the expression.
- When you remove brackets in part of an expression you may end up with like terms. Add or subtract any like terms to simplify the expression fully.
- In general terms $a(b + c) = ab + ac$

Exercise 2.4

Remember the rules for multiplying integers:

$+ \times + = +$

$- \times - = +$

$+ \times - = -$

If the quantity in front of a bracket is negative, the signs of the terms inside the bracket will change when the brackets are expanded.

1 Expand.

(a) $3(x + 2)$ **(b)** $2(x - 4)$ **(c)** $-2(x + 3)$ **(d)** $-3(3 - 2x)$

(e) $x(x + 3)$ **(f)** $x(2 - x)$ **(g)** $-x(2 + 2x)$ **(h)** $3x(x - 3)$

(i) $-2x(2 - 5x)$ **(j)** $-(x - 2)$ **(k)** $-2x(2y - 2x)$ **(l)** $-x(2x - 4)$

2 Remove the brackets and simplify where possible.

(a) $2x(x - 2)$ **(b)** $(y - 3)x$ **(c)** $(x - 2) - 3x$ **(d)** $-2x - (x - 2)$

(e) $(x - 3)(-2x)$ **(f)** $2(x + 1) - (1 - x)$ **(g)** $x(x^2 - 2x - 1)$

(h) $-x(1 - x) + 2(x + 3) - 4$

3 Remove the brackets and simplify where possible.

(a) $2x\left(\tfrac{1}{2}x + \tfrac{1}{4}\right)$ **(b)** $-3x(x - y) - 2x(y - 2x)$ **(c)** $-2\left(4x^2 - 2x - 1\right)x$

(d) $(x + y) - \left(\tfrac{1}{2}x - \tfrac{1}{2}y\right)$ **(e)** $2x(2x - 2) - x(x + 2)$ **(f)** $x(1 - x) + x(2x - 5) - 2x(1 + 3x)$

2.5 Indices

- An index (also called a power or exponent) shows how many times the base is multiplied by itself.
- x^2 means $x \times x$ and $(3y)^4$ means $3y \times 3y \times 3y \times 3y$.
- The laws of indices are used to simplify algebraic terms and expressions. Make sure you know the laws and understand how they work (see below).
- When an expression contains negative indices you apply the same laws as for other indices to simplify it.

Tip

Memorise this summary of the **index laws:**

1. $x^m \times x^n = x^{m+n}$ (1)
2. $x^m \div x^n = x^{m-n}$ (2)
3. $(x^m)^n = x^{mn}$ (3)
4. $x^0 = 1$ (4)
5. $x^{-m} = \dfrac{1}{x^m}$ (5)

Remember, a fraction is the top value divided by the bottom value. This means $\dfrac{x^m}{x^n}$ is the same as $x^m \div x^n$ so you can use the second index law to simplify it.

Tip

Apply the index laws and work in this order:

- simplify any terms in brackets
- apply the multiplication law (1 above) to numerators and then to denominators
- cancel numbers if you can
- apply the division law (2 above) if the same letter appears in the numerator and denominator
- express your answer using positive indices

Exercise 2.5 A

1 Simplify.

(a) $x^9 \times x^2$ (b) $y^{10} \times y^3$ (c) $2x \times 3x^2$ (d) $-2x^2 \times -3x^6$

(e) $x^2 y^3 \times x^3 y$ (f) $-2x \times 8x \times -3x^2$ (g) $\left(2x^2 y\right)\left(xy\right)$ (h) $-3x^4 \times 9x^8$

2 Simplify.

(a) $2x^5 \div 3x^3$ (b) $18x^3 yz^2 \div 6xyz^2$ (c) $12xy^3 \div 18xy^2$ (d) $-6x \div -12x^2$

(e) $21x^2 y \div 14x^4 y^6$ (f) $\dfrac{12x^3 yz^2}{6xy^4 z}$ (g) $\dfrac{14x^2}{2x^3}$ (h) $\dfrac{16x^2 y}{4xy^2}$

(i) $\dfrac{x^2 y}{3xy^2}$ (j) $\dfrac{x^7 y^3}{x^4 y^5}$ (k) $\dfrac{36x^2 yz^4}{-24xyz}$ (l) $\dfrac{9x^3 y^{-2}}{18x^{-2} y^4}$

3 Rewrite each of the following using positive indices only.

(a) 3^{-2} (b) $3x^{-3}$ (c) $\dfrac{xy^{-1}}{2}$

(d) $\left(xy\right)^{-1}$ (e) $\left(8xy\right)^{-2}$ (f) $\dfrac{1}{\left(4xy\right)^{-2}}$

(g) $y^{-5} \times y^6$ (h) $x^3 y^{-1} \times y^{-3}$ (i) $x^3 y \times x^{-1} y^{-3}$

(j) $y^6 \left(x^3\right)^{-4} \times \left(x^3 y^{-2}\right)^2$ (k) $\left(3xy^3\right)^{-2} \times \left(2x^3 y\right)^3$ (l) $\dfrac{4y^{-2}}{7x^{-3}}$

4 Simplify.

(a) $\left(x^3\right)^2$ (b) $\left(-2x^3\right)^3$ (c) $\left(\dfrac{2x^2}{x}\right)^4$ (d) $\left(x^9\right)^3$

(e) $\left(-xy^2\right)^9$ (f) $\left(x^3 y^2\right)^4$ (g) $-2\left(xy\right)^3$ (h) $2x^2 \left(2x\right)^3$

(i) $\dfrac{\left(xy^2\right)^3}{x^3 y^6}$ (j) $\left(xy\right)^4 \left(x^4\right)^3$ (k) $\left(3x^y\right)^y$ (l) $-\left(2x^2\right)^3$

Exercise 2.5 B

1 Simplify.

(a) $\dfrac{x^4 y \times y^2 x^6}{x^4 y^5}$ (b) $\dfrac{2x^2 y^4 \times 3x^3 y}{2xy^4}$ (c) $\dfrac{2x^5 y^4 \times 2xy^3}{2x^2 y^5 \times 3x^2 y^3}$

(d) $\dfrac{x^3 y^7}{xy^4} \times \dfrac{x^2 y^8}{x^3 y}$ (e) $\dfrac{2x^7 y^2}{4x^3 y^7} \times \dfrac{10x^8 y^4}{2x^3 y^2}$ (f) $\dfrac{x^9 y^6}{x^4 y^2} \div \dfrac{x^3 y^2}{x^5 y}$

Tip

Some exam questions will accept simplified expressions with negative indices, such as $5x^{-4}$. If, however, the question states positive indices only, you can use the law $x^{-m} = \dfrac{1}{x^m}$ so that $5x^{-4} = \dfrac{5}{x^4}$.

Similarly, $\dfrac{y}{x^{-2}} = x^2 y$.

(g) $\dfrac{10x^5 y^2}{9x^6 y^6} \div \dfrac{3x^3 y}{5x^7 y^4}$

(h) $\dfrac{7y^3 x^2}{5y^5 x^4} \div \dfrac{5x^6 y^2}{7x^5 y^3}$

(i) $\dfrac{\left(x^5 y\right)^2 \times \left(x^3 y^4\right)^2}{\left(x^3 y^3\right)^3}$

(j) $\dfrac{\left(2x^4 y^2\right)^3}{\left(y^3 x^2\right)^3} \times \dfrac{\left(x^4 y^4\right)^2}{3\left(x^2 y\right)^2}$

(k) $\left(\dfrac{x^2}{y^4}\right)^3 \times \left(\dfrac{x^5}{y^2}\right)^2$

(l) $\dfrac{\left(5x^3 y^2\right)^3}{4x^7 y^6} \div \left(\dfrac{2xy^3}{5x^2 y^4}\right)^2$

2 Simplify each expression and give your answer using positive indices only.

(a) $\dfrac{x^5 y^{-4}}{x^{-3} y^{-2}}$

(b) $\dfrac{x^{-4} y^3}{x^2 y^{-1}} \times \dfrac{x^7 y^{-5}}{x^{-4} y^3}$

(c) $\dfrac{\left(2x^{-3} y^{-1}\right)^3}{\left(y^2 x^{-2}\right)^2}$

(d) $\left(\dfrac{x}{y^3}\right)^{-1} \div \dfrac{\left(x^2\right)^4}{y^{-3}}$

(e) $\dfrac{x^{-10}}{\left(y^{-4}\right)^2} \div \left(\dfrac{y^2}{x^3}\right)^{-4}$

(f) $\left(\dfrac{x^4 y^{-1}}{x^5 y^{-3}}\right)^2 \times \dfrac{\left(x^{-2} y^6\right)^2}{2\left(xy^3\right)^{-2}}$

Mixed exercise

1 Write each of the following as an algebraic expression. Use x to represent 'the number'.

(a) A number increased by 12.

(b) A number decreased by four.

(c) Five times a number.

(d) A number divided by three.

(e) The product of a number and four.

(f) A quarter of a number.

(g) A number subtracted from 12.

(h) The difference between a number and its cube.

2 Determine the value of $x^2 - 5x$ if:

(a) $x = 2$

(b) $x = -3$

(c) $x = \frac{1}{3}$

3 Evaluate each expression if $a = -1$, $b = 2$ and $c = 0$.

(a) $\dfrac{-2a + 3b}{2ab}$

(b) $\dfrac{b(c - a)}{b - a}$

(c) $\dfrac{a - b^2}{c - a^2}$

(d) $\dfrac{3 - 2(a - 1)}{c - a(b - 1)}$

(e) $a^3 b^2 - 2a^2 + a^4 b^2 - ac^3$

4 (a) $M = 9ab$. Find M when $a = 7$ and $b = 10$.

(b) $V - rs = 2uw$. Find V when $r = 8$, $s = 4$, $u = 6$ and $w = 1$.

(c) $\dfrac{V}{30} = \sqrt{h}$. Find V when $h = 25$.

(d) $P - y = x^2$. Find P when $x = 2$ and $y = 8$.

5 Remove the brackets and simplify as fully as possible.

(a) $2(y + 5)$

(b) $4(y - 1)$

(c) $3(2x + 5)$

(d) $4(3x - 2y)$

(e) $x(y + 2)$

(f) $2(10x - 7y + 3z)$

(g) $2x(3x + 1)$

(h) $2(x + 3) + 1$

(i) $6(x + 3) - 2x$

(j) $3x + 2(6x - 3y)$

6 Simplify each of the following expressions as fully as possible.

(a) $3a + 4b + 6a - 3b$

(b) $x^2 + 4x - x - 2$

(c) $-2a^2b(2a^2 - 3b^2)$

(d) $2x(x-3)-(x-4)-2x^2$

(e) $16x^2y \div 4y^2x$

(f) $\dfrac{10x^2 - 5xy}{2x}$

7 Expand and simplify if possible.

(a) $2(4x-3)+3(x+1)$

(b) $3x(2x+3)-2(4-3x)$

(c) $x(x+2)+3x-3(x^2-4)$

(d) $x^2(x+3)-2x^3-(x-5)$

8 Simplify. Give all answers with positive indices only.

(a) $\dfrac{15x^7}{18x^2}$

(b) $5x^2 \times \dfrac{3x^5}{x^7}$

(c) $\dfrac{\left(x^3\right)^4}{\left(x^2\right)^8}$

(d) $\left(2xy^2\right)^4$

(e) $\left(\dfrac{4x^3}{y^5}\right)^3$

(f) $\left(x^3y\right)^2 \times \dfrac{\left(x^2y^4\right)^3}{\left(xy^2\right)^3}$

(g) $\left(2xy^3\right)^{-2} \times \left(3x^2y\right)^3$

(h) $\dfrac{\left(x^{-3}y^2\right)^4}{2\left(xy^2\right)^{-3}} \div \left(\dfrac{x^{-3}y^3}{x^2y^{-1}}\right)^2$

3 Lines, angles and shapes

3.1 Lines and angles

- Angles can be classified according to their size:
  - acute angles are $< 90°$
  - right angles are $90°$
  - obtuse angles are $> 90°$ but $< 180°$
  - reflex angles are $> 180°$ but $< 360°$.
- Two angles that add up to $90°$ are called complementary angles. Two angles that add up to $180°$ are called supplementary angles.
- The sum of adjacent angles on a straight line is $180°$.
- The sum of the angles around a point is $360°$.
- When two lines intersect (cross), two pairs of vertically opposite angles are formed. Vertically opposite angles are equal.
- When two parallel lines are cut by a transversal, alternate angles are equal, corresponding angles are equal and co-interior angles add up to $180°$.
- When alternate or corresponding angles are equal, or when co-interior angles add up to $180°$, the lines are parallel.

Exercise 3.1 A

1 Estimate the size of each angle and say what type of angle it is. Then measure each angle with a protractor and give its size in degrees.

(a)    (b)   (c)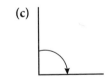

(d) 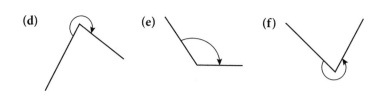 **(e)** **(f)**

2 Look at the clock face on the left. Calculate the following.

    (a) The angle between the hands of the clock at:

        (i) 3 a.m.   **(ii)** 1800 hours.

    (b) Through how many degrees does the hour hand move between 4 p.m. and 5 p.m.?

    (c) Through how many degrees does the minute hand turn in one hour?

    (d) A clock shows 12 noon. What will the time be when the minute hand has moved 270° clockwise?

3 Will doubling an acute angle always produce an obtuse angle? Explain your answer.

4 Will halving an obtuse angle always produce an acute angle? Explain your answer.

5 What is the complement of each the following angles?

    (a) 45°   **(b)** 62°   **(c)** $x°$ **(d)** $(90 - x)°$

6 What is the supplement of each of the following angles?

    (a) 45°   **(b)** 90°   **(c)** 104°   **(d)** $x°$

    (e) $(180 - x)°$ **(f)** $(90 - x)°$ **(g)** $(90 + x)°$ **(h)** $(2x - 40)$

> **! Tip**
>
> You need to be able to use the relationships between lines and angles to calculate the values of unknown angles.

Exercise 3.1 B

In this exercise, calculate (do not measure from the diagrams) the values of the lettered angles. You should also state your reasons.

1 In the following diagram, *PQ* and *RS* are straight lines. Calculate the sizes of angles *x*, *y* and *z*.

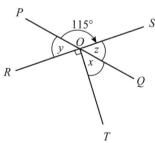

> Remember, give reasons for statements. Use these abbreviations:
>
> Comp ∠s
> Supp ∠s
> ∠s on line
> ∠s round point
> VO ∠s

2 In the following diagram, *MN* and *PQ* are straight lines. Find the size of angle *a*.

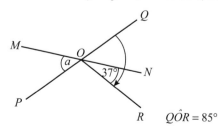

$Q\hat{O}R = 85°$

3 Calculate the value of x in each of the following figures.

(a)

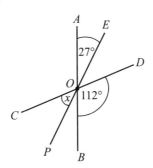

(b)

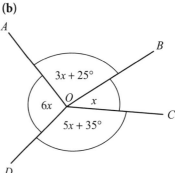

Exercise 3.1 C

1 In this figure the size of angle AGH is given. Calculate the size of all the other angles giving reasons.

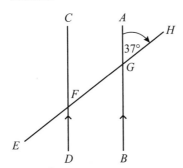

2 Find the values of the angles marked with letters in each diagram. Give reasons for any statements you make.

(a)

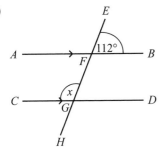

(b)

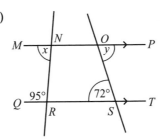

(c)

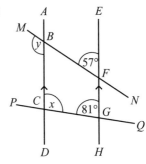

(d)

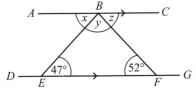

(e)

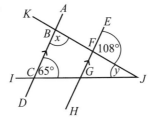

(f)

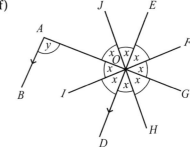

3 Calculate the value of *x* and *y* in each of the following figures. Give reasons for your answers.

(a)

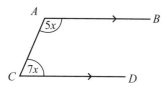

(b)

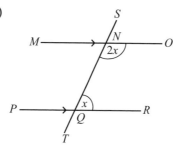

(c)

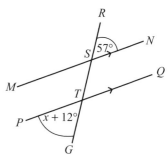

(d)

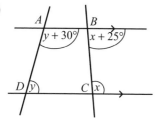

(e)

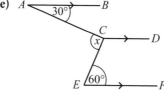

(f)

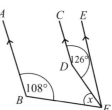

3.2 Triangles

- Scalene triangles have no equal sides and no equal angles.
- Isosceles triangles have two equal sides. The angles at the bases of the equal sides are equal in size. The converse is also true – if a triangle has two equal angles, then it is isosceles.
- Equilateral triangles have three equal sides and three equal angles (each being 60°).
- The sum of the interior angles of any triangle is 180°.
- The exterior angle of a triangle is equal to the sum of the two opposite interior angles.

Exercise 3.2

REWIND

You may also need to apply the angle relationships for points, lines and parallel lines to find the missing angles in triangles. ◀

1 Find the angles marked with letters. Give reasons for any statements.

(a)

(b)

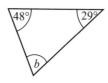

(c)

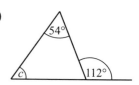

(d)

(e)

(f)

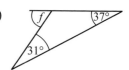

(g)

(h)

(i)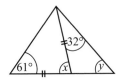

(j)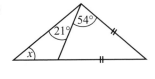

(k)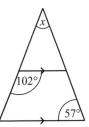

(l)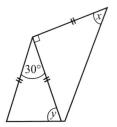

2 Calculate the value of x and hence find the size of the marked angles.

(a)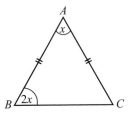

(b)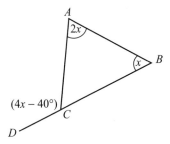

(c)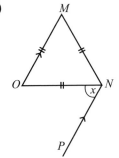

(d)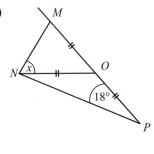

(e)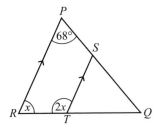

(f)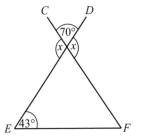

3.3 Quadrilaterals

- A quadrilateral is a four-sided shape.
  - A trapezium has one pair of parallel sides.
  - A kite has two pairs of adjacent sides equal in length. The diagonals intersect at 90° and the longer diagonal bisects the shorter one. Only one pair of opposite angles is equal. The diagonals bisect the opposite angles.
  - A parallelogram has opposite sides equal and parallel. The opposite angles are equal in size and the diagonals bisect each other.
  - A rectangle has opposite sides equal and parallel and interior angles each equal to 90°. The diagonals are equal in length and they bisect each other.
  - A rhombus is a parallelogram with all four sides equal in length. The diagonals bisect each other at 90° and bisect the opposite angles.
  - A square has four equal sides and four angles each equal to 90°. The opposite sides are parallel. The diagonals are equal in length, they bisect each other at right angles and they bisect the opposite angles.
- The sum of the interior angles of a quadrilateral is 360°.

Exercise 3.3

REWIND

The angle relationships for parallel lines will apply when a quadrilateral has parallel sides. ◀

1 Each of the following statements applies to one or more quadrilaterals. For each one, name the quadrilateral(s) to which it always applies.

- **(a)** All sides are equal in length
- **(b)** All angles are equal in size
- **(c)** The diagonals are the same length
- **(d)** The diagonals bisect each other
- **(e)** The angles are all 90° and the diagonals bisect each other
- **(f)** Opposite angles are equal in size
- **(g)** The diagonals intersect at right angles
- **(h)** The diagonals bisect the opposite angles
- **(i)** One diagonal divides the quadrilateral into two isosceles triangles

2 Calculate the size of the marked angles in the following figures. Give reasons or state the properties you are using.

(a)

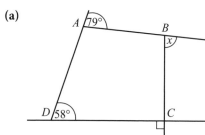

(b)

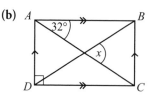

(c)

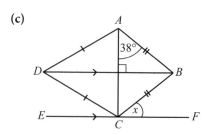

(d)

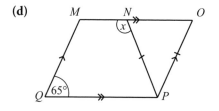

(e)

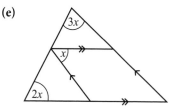

(f)

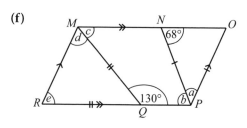

3.4 Polygons

- A polygon is a two-dimensional shape with three or more sides. Polygons are named according the number of sides they have:
  - – triangle (3)
  - – quadrilateral (4)
  - – pentagon (5)
  - – hexagon (6)
  - – heptagon (7)
  - – octagon (8)
  - – nonagon (9)
  - – decagon (10).

- A regular polygon has all its sides equal and all its angles equal.
- The interior angle sum of any polygon can be worked out using the formula $(n - 2) \times 180°$ where n is the number of sides. Once you have the angle sum, you can find the size of one angle of a regular polygon by dividing the total by the number of angles.
- The sum of the exterior angles of any convex polygon is 360°.

Exercise 3.4

Tip

If you can't remember the formula, you can find the size of one interior angle of a regular polygon using the fact that the exterior angles add up to 360°. Divide 360 by the number of angles to find the size of one exterior angle. Then use the fact that the exterior and interior angles form a straight line (180°) to work out the size of the interior angle.

1 For a regular hexagon.

    (a) Calculate the size on one exterior angle.

    (b) Find the sum of the interior angles.

    (c) What is the size of each interior angle?

2 Find the sum of the interior angles of:

    (a) a regular octagon

    (b) a regular decagon

    (c) a regular 15-sided polygon.

3 A coin is made in the shape of a regular 7-sided polygon. Calculate the size of each interior angle.

4 The interior angle of a regular polygon is 162°. How many sides does the polygon have?

5 One exterior angle of a regular polygon is 14.4°.

    (a) What is the size of each interior angle?

    (b) How many sides does the polygon have?

3.5 Circles

- A circle is a set of points equidistant from a fixed centre. Half a circle is a semi-circle.
- The perimeter of a circle is called its circumference.
- The distance across a circle (through the centre) is called its diameter. A radius is half a diameter.
- An arc is part of the circumference of a circle.
- A chord is a line joining two points on the circumference. A chord cuts the circle into two segments.
- A 'slice' of a circle, made by two radii and the arc between them on the circumference, is called a sector.
- A tangent is a line that touches a circle at only one point.

Exercise 3.5

Copy and complete the table below, naming each part of the circle and giving its definition.

Diagram	Name	Definition

Diagram	Name	Definition

3.6 Construction

- You need to be able to use a ruler and a pair of compasses to construct triangles (given the lengths of three sides) and bisect lines and angles. You also need to be able to construct other simple geometric figures from given specifications.
- The diagrams below show you how to bisect an angle and how to draw the perpendicular bisector of a line:

How to bisect an angle.

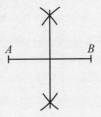

How to draw the perpendicular bisector of a line.

Tip

! Always start with a rough sketch. Label your rough sketch so you know what lengths you need to measure.

Exercise 3.6

1 Draw angle $ABC = 75°$. Accurately bisect the angle.

2 Construct $\triangle ABC$ with $AC = 7\,cm$, $CB = 6\,cm$ and $AB = 8\,cm$.

3 Construct $\triangle MNO$ with $MN = 4.5\,cm$, $NO = 5.5\,cm$ and $MO = 8\,cm$. Construct the perpendicular bisector of NO. Label the bisected point X and extend the line to cut MO at Y. Measure the length of XY to the nearest millimetre.

4 Construct $\triangle DEF$ with $DE = 100\,mm$, $FE = 70\,mm$ and $DF = 50\,mm$.

   (a) What type of triangle is DEF?
   (b) Bisect each angle of the triangle. Do the angle bisectors meet at the same point?

5 Accurately construct a square of side 4.7 cm. What is the length of a diagonal of the square?

Mixed exercise

1 Write a correct mathematical definition for each of the following:

   (a) alternate angles
   (b) an isosceles triangle
   (c) a kite
   (d) a rhombus
   (e) a regular polygon
   (f) an octagon.

2 Find the value of the marked angles in each of the following.

(a)
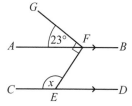

(b)
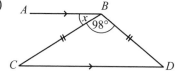

(c)
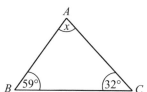

(d)
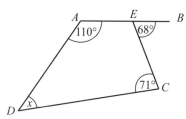

(e)
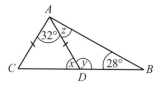

(f)
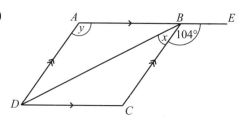

(g)
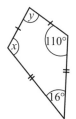

(h)

3 For each shape combination find the size of angle *x*. All shapes in both figures are regular polygons.

(a)

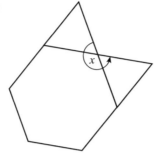

(b)

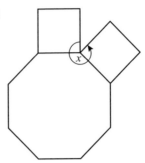

4 Use the diagram of the circle with centre *O* to answer these questions.

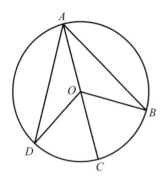

  (a) What are the correct mathematical names for:
    (i) *DO*   **(ii)** *AB*   **(iii)** *AC*?
  (b) Four radii are shown on the diagram. Name them.
  (c) If *OB* is 12.4 cm long, how long is *AC*?
  (d) Draw a copy of the circle and on to it draw the tangent to the circle that passes through point *B*.

5 Use a ruler and a protractor to draw line segment *AB* 11 cm long. Construct *XY*, the perpendicular bisector of *AB* with point *X* on *AB*. Bisect angle *BXY*.

6 Construct $\triangle ABC$ with $AB = BC = AC = 6.5$ cm. Construct the perpendicular bisector of *AB*. Where does this intersect with the triangle?

Collecting, organising and displaying data

4.1 Collecting and classifying data

- Data is a set of facts, numbers or other information, collected to try to answer a question.
- Primary data is 'original' data and can be collected by measuring, observation, doing experiments, carrying out surveys or asking people to complete questionnaires.
- Secondary data is data drawn from a non-original source. For example you could find the area of each of the world's oceans by referring to an atlas.
- You can classify data as qualitative or quantitative.
- Qualitative data is non-numeric such as colour, make of vehicle or favourite flavour.
- Quantitative data is numerical data that was counted or measured. For example age, marks in a test, shoe size, height.
- Quantitative data can be discrete or continuous.
- Discrete data can only take certain values and is usually something counted. For example, the number of children in your family. There are no in-between values; you can't have $2\frac{1}{2}$ children in a family.
- Continuous data can take any value and is usually something measured. For example the heights of trees in a rainforest could range from 50 to 60 metres. Any value in-between those two heights is possible.

Exercise 4.1

The following table of data was collected about ten students in a high school. Study the table and then answer the questions about the data.

Student	1	2	3	4	5	6	7	8	9	10
Gender	F	F	M	M	M	F	M	F	F	M
Height (m)	1.55	1.61	1.63	1.60	1.61	1.62	1.64	1.69	1.61	1.65
Shoe size	3	4	7	6	9	7	8	7	5	10
Mass (kg)	40	51	52	54	60	43	55	56	51	55
Eye colour	Br	Gr	Gr	Br	Br	Br	Br	Gr	Bl	Br
Hair colour	Bl	Bl	Blo	Br	Br	Br	Bl	Bl	Bl	Bl
No. of brothers/ sisters	0	3	4	2	1	2	3	1	0	3

(a) Which of these data categories are qualitative?

(b) Which of these data categories are quantitative?

(c) Which sets of numerical data are discrete data?

(d) Which sets of numerical data are continuous data?

(e) How do you think each set of data was collected? Give a reason for your answers.

4.2 Organising data

- Once data has been collected, it needs to be arranged and organised so that it is easier to work with, interpret and make inferences about.
- Tally tables and frequency tables are used to organise data and to show the totals of different values or categories.
- When you have a large set of numerical data, with lots of different scores, you can group the data into intervals called class intervals. Class intervals should not overlap.
- A two way table can be used to show the frequency of results for two or more sets of data.

Exercise 4.2

In data handling, the word **frequency** means the number of times a score or observation occurs.

1 Here are the marks obtained by 40 students in an assignment. The assignment was out of 10.

6	5	6	7	4	5	8	6	7	10
7	6	5	6	1	9	4	4	2	6
5	5	7	3	4	5	8	3	5	8
10	9	9	7	5	5	7	6	4	2

Copy and complete this tally table to organise the data.

Mark	Tally	Frequency
1		
2		
⋮	⋮	⋮

2 Nika tossed a dice 40 times and got these results.

6	6	6	5	4	3	2	6	5	4
1	1	3	2	5	4	3	3	3	2
1	6	5	5	4	4	3	2	5	4
6	3	2	4	2	1	2	2	1	5

(a) Copy and complete this frequency table to organise the data.

Score	1	2	3	4	5	6
Frequency						

(b) Do the results suggest that this is a fair dice or not? Give a reason for your answer.

3 These are the percentage scores of 50 students in an examination.

54	26	60	40	55	82	67	59	57	70
67	44	63	56	46	48	55	63	42	58
45	54	76	65	63	61	49	54	54	53
67	56	69	57	38	57	51	55	59	78
65	52	55	78	69	71	73	88	80	91

Score	Frequency
0–29	
30–39	
40–49	
50–59	
60–69	
70–79	
80–100	

(a) Copy and complete this grouped frequency table to organise the results.

(b) How many students scored 70% or more?

(c) How many students scored lower than 40%?

(d) How many students scored 40% or more but less than 60%?

(e) The first and last class interval in the table are greater than the others. Suggest why this is the case.

4 This is a section of the table you worked with in Exercise 4.1.

Student	1	2	3	4	5	6	7	8	9	10
Gender	F	F	M	M	M	F	M	F	F	M
Eye colour	Br	Gr	Gr	Br	Br	Br	Br	Gr	Bl	Br
Hair colour	Bl	Bl	Blo	Br	Br	Br	Bl	Bl	Bl	Bl
No. of siblings (brothers/sisters)	0	3	4	2	1	2	3	1	0	3

(a) Copy and complete this two way table using data from the table.

Eye colour	Brown	Blue	Green
Male			
Female			

(b) Draw up and complete two similar two way tables of your own to show the hair colour and number of brothers or sisters by gender.

(c) Write a sentence to summarise what you found out for each table.

4.3 Using charts to display data

- Charts usually help you to see patterns and trends in data more easily than in tables.
- Pictograms use symbols to show the frequency of data in different categories. They are useful for discrete, categorical and ungrouped data.
- Bar charts are useful for categorical and ungrouped data. A bar chart has bars of equal width which are equally spaced.
- Bar charts can be drawn as horizontal or vertical charts. They can also show two or more sets of data on the same set of axes.
- Pie charts are circular graphs that use sectors of circle to show the proportion of data in each category.
- All charts should have a heading and clearly labelled scales, axes or keys.

Exercise 4.3

1 Study the diagram carefully and answer the questions about it.

Number of students in each year

Key
= 30 students

(a) What type of chart is this?

(b) What does the chart show?

(c) What does each full symbol represent?

(d) How are 15 students shown on the chart?

(e) How many students are there in year 8?

(f) Which year group has the most students? How many are there in this year group?

(g) Do you think these are accurate or rounded figures? Why?

2 The table shows the population (in millions) of five of the world's largest cities.

City	Tokyo	Seoul	Mexico City	New York	Mumbai
Population (millions)	32.5	20.6	20.5	19.75	19.2

Draw a pictogram to show this data.

3 Study the two bar charts below.

(a) What does chart A show?
(b) How many boys are there in Class 10A?
(c) How many students are there in 10A altogether?
(d) What does chart B show?
(e) Which sport is most popular with boys?
(f) Which sport is most popular with girls?
(g) How many students chose basketball as their favourite sport?

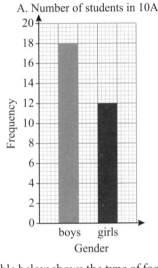

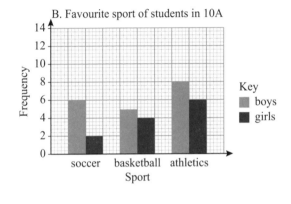

4 The table below shows the type of food that a group of students in a hostel chose for breakfast.

	Cereal	Hot porridge	Bread
Girls	8	16	12
Boys	2	12	10

(a) Draw a single bar chart to show the choice of cereal against bread.
(b) Draw a compound bar chart to show the breakfast food choice for girls and boys.

5 Jyoti recorded the number and type of 180 vehicles passing her home in Bangalore. She drew this pie chart to show her results.

Traffic passing my home

(a) Which type of vehicle was most common?
(b) What percentage of the vehicles were tuk-tuks?
(c) How many trucks passed Jyoti's home?
(d) Which types of vehicles were least common?

6 In an IGCSE exam the results for 120 students were: 5% attained an A grade, 12% attained a B grade, 41% attained a C grade, 25% attained a D grade and the rest attained E grade or lower.

(a) Represent this information on a pie chart.
(b) How many students attained an A?
(c) How many students attained a D or lower?
(d) Which grade was attained by most of the students?

Mixed exercise

1 Mika collected data about how many children different families in her community had. These are her results.

0	3	4	3	3	2	2	2	2	1	1	1
3	3	4	3	6	2	2	2	0	0	2	1
5	4	3	2	4	3	3	3	2	1	1	0
3	1	1	1	1	0	0	0	2	4	5	3

(a) How do you think Mika collected the data?
(b) Is this data discrete or continuous? Why?
(c) Is this data qualitative or quantitative? Why?
(d) Draw up a frequency table, with tallies, to organise the data.
(e) Represent the data on a pie chart.
(f) Draw a bar chart to compare the number of families that have three or fewer children with those that have four or more children.

2 Mrs Sanchez bakes and sells cookies. One week she sells 420 peanut crunchies, 488 chocolate cups and 320 coconut munchies. Draw a pictogram to represent this data.

3 Study the chart in the margin.

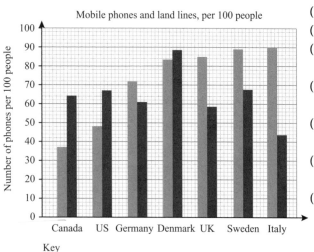

Mobile phones and land lines, per 100 people

Number of phones per 100 people

Canada   US   Germany   Denmark   UK   Sweden   Italy

Key
■ Mobile phones   ■ Land lines

(a) What do you call this type of chart?
(b) What does the chart show?
(c) Can you tell how many people in each country have a mobile phone from this chart? Explain your answer.
(d) In which countries do a greater proportion of the people have a land line than a mobile phone?
(e) In which countries do more people have mobile phones than land lines?
(f) In which country do more than 80% of the population have a land line and a mobile phone?
(g) What do you think the bars would look like for your country? Why?

5 Fractions

5.1 Equivalent fractions

- Equivalent means, 'has the same value'.
- To find equivalent fractions either multiply both the numerator and denominator by the same number or divide both the numerator and denominator by the same number.

You can cross multiply to make an equation and then solve it. For example:

$$\frac{1}{2} \diagdown \frac{x}{28}$$

$2x = 28$

$x = 14$

Exercise 5.1

1 Write each fraction in its simplest form.

(a) $\dfrac{6}{12}$ (b) $\dfrac{4}{12}$ (c) $\dfrac{3}{9}$ (d) $\dfrac{8}{32}$ (e) $\dfrac{12}{48}$

(f) $\dfrac{125}{1000}$ (g) $\dfrac{3}{15}$ (h) $\dfrac{4}{6}$ (i) $\dfrac{24}{32}$ (j) $\dfrac{375}{1000}$

2 Find the missing value in each pair of equivalent fractions.

(a) $\dfrac{3}{4} = \dfrac{x}{44}$ (b) $\dfrac{1}{3} = \dfrac{x}{900}$ (c) $\dfrac{1}{2} = \dfrac{x}{50}$ (d) $\dfrac{2}{5} = \dfrac{26}{x}$ (e) $\dfrac{5}{7} = \dfrac{120}{x}$

(f) $\dfrac{6}{5} = \dfrac{66}{x}$ (g) $\dfrac{11}{9} = \dfrac{143}{x}$ (h) $\dfrac{5}{3} = \dfrac{80}{x}$ (i) $\dfrac{8}{12} = \dfrac{x}{156}$ (j) $\dfrac{7}{9} = \dfrac{49}{x}$

5.2 Operations on fractions

- To multiply fractions, multiply numerators by numerators and denominators by denominators. Mixed numbers should be rewritten as improper fractions before multiplying or dividing.
- To add or subtract fractions change them to equivalent fractions with the same denominator, then add (or subtract) the numerators only.
- To divide by a fraction, invert the fraction (turn it upside down) and change the ÷ sign to a × sign.
- Unless you are specifically asked for a mixed number, give answers to calculations with fractions as proper or improper fractions in their simplest form.

> **! Tip**
> If you can simplify the fraction part first you will have smaller numbers to multiply to get the improper fraction.

Exercise 5.2

1 Rewrite each mixed number as an improper fraction in its simplest form.

(a) $2\dfrac{7}{42}$ (b) $3\dfrac{5}{40}$ (c) $1\dfrac{12}{22}$ (d) $9\dfrac{30}{100}$ (e) $11\dfrac{24}{30}$

(f) $3\dfrac{75}{100}$ (g) $14\dfrac{3}{4}$ (h) $2\dfrac{35}{45}$ (i) $9\dfrac{15}{45}$ (j) $-2\dfrac{7}{9}$

Remember, you can cancel to simplify when you are multiplying fractions.

2 Multiply, giving your answers in simplest form.

(a) $\frac{1}{5} \times \frac{3}{15}$ (b) $\frac{1}{4} \times \frac{2}{5}$ (c) $\frac{2}{3} \times \frac{6}{10}$ (d) $\frac{3}{5} \times \frac{9}{12}$ (e) $\frac{2}{11} \times \frac{8}{9}$

(f) $\frac{6}{11} \times \frac{2}{3}$ (g) $\frac{10}{13} \times \frac{3}{7}$ (h) $\frac{20}{50} \times \frac{9}{15}$ (i) $\frac{10}{14} \times \frac{3}{4}$ (j) $\frac{6}{8} \times \frac{3}{11}$

Remember, the word 'of' means ×.

3 Calculate.

(a) $1\frac{4}{5} \times 12$ (b) $\frac{9}{13} \times 7$ (c) $3\frac{1}{2} \times 4$ (d) $2\frac{1}{3} \times 2\frac{2}{5}$

(e) $2 \times 4\frac{1}{2} \times \frac{1}{3}$ (f) $\frac{1}{5} \times \frac{12}{19} \times 2\frac{1}{2}$ (g) $\frac{1}{3}$ of 360 (h) $\frac{3}{4}$ of $\frac{2}{7}$

(i) $\frac{8}{9}$ of 81 (j) $\frac{2}{3}$ of $4\frac{1}{2}$ (k) $\frac{1}{2}$ of $9\frac{16}{50}$ (l) $\frac{3}{4}$ of $2\frac{1}{3}$

4 Calculate, giving your answer as a fraction in simplest form.

(a) $\frac{3}{4} - \frac{1}{5}$ (b) $\frac{1}{5} + \frac{1}{6}$ (c) $\frac{1}{5} - \frac{1}{9}$ (d) $\frac{1}{6} + \frac{3}{8}$

(e) $\frac{2}{3} - \frac{4}{10}$ (f) $\frac{9}{10} - \frac{7}{12}$ (g) $\frac{4}{7} + \frac{1}{3}$ (h) $\frac{2}{3} + \frac{2}{5}$

(i) $\frac{7}{8} - \frac{1}{3}$ (j) $2\frac{1}{2} + 3\frac{1}{3}$ (k) $2\frac{1}{8} + 1\frac{1}{7}$ (l) $4\frac{3}{10} + 3\frac{3}{4}$

(m) $1\frac{1}{13} - \frac{4}{5}$ (n) $3\frac{9}{10} - 2\frac{7}{8}$ (o) $2\frac{5}{7} - 1\frac{1}{3}$ (p) $1\frac{1}{2} - \frac{7}{3}$

(q) $2\frac{1}{3} - \frac{17}{3}$ (r) $1\frac{4}{9} - \frac{13}{3}$ (s) $2\frac{1}{3} - \frac{12}{7}$ (t) $9\frac{1}{4} - \frac{17}{3}$

Tip

You can use any common denominator but it is easier to simplify if you use the lowest one.

5 Calculate.

(a) $8 \div \frac{1}{3}$ (b) $12 \div \frac{7}{8}$ (c) $\frac{7}{8} \div 12$

(d) $\frac{2}{9} \div \frac{18}{30}$ (e) $\frac{8}{9} \div \frac{4}{5}$ (f) $1\frac{3}{7} \div 2\frac{2}{9}$

REWIND

The order of operations rules (BODMAS) that were covered in chapter 1 apply here too. ◄

6 Simplify the following.

(a) $4 + \frac{2}{3} \times \frac{1}{3}$ (b) $2\frac{1}{8} - \left(2\frac{1}{5} - \frac{7}{8}\right)$ (c) $\frac{3}{7} \times \left(\frac{2}{3} + 6 \div \frac{2}{3}\right) + 5 \times \frac{2}{7}$

(d) $2\frac{7}{8} + \left(8\frac{1}{4} - 6\frac{3}{8}\right)$ (e) $\frac{5}{6} \times \frac{1}{4} + \frac{5}{8} \times \frac{1}{3}$ (f) $\left(5 \div \frac{3}{11} - \frac{5}{12}\right) \times \frac{1}{6}$

(g) $\left(\frac{5}{8} \div \frac{15}{4}\right) - \left(\frac{5}{6} \times \frac{1}{5}\right)$ (h) $\left(2\frac{2}{3} \div 4 - \frac{3}{10}\right) \times \frac{3}{17}$ (i) $\left(7 \div \frac{2}{9} - \frac{1}{3}\right) \times \frac{2}{3}$

7 Mrs West has $900 dollars in her account. She spends $\frac{7}{12}$ of this.

(a) How much does she spend?

(b) How much does she have left?

8 It takes a builder $\frac{3}{4}$ of an hour to lay 50 tiles.

(a) How many tiles will he lay in $4\frac{1}{2}$ hours?

(b) If the builder lays tiles at the same rate for $6\frac{3}{4}$ hours a day, five days a week, how many tiles will he lay during the week?

5.3 Percentages

- Per cent means per hundred. A percentage is a fraction with a denominator of 100.
- To write one quantity as a percentage of another, express it as a fraction and then convert to a percentage by multiplying by 100.
- To find a percentage of a quantity, multiply the percentage by the quantity.
- To increase or decrease an amount by a percentage, find the percentage amount and add or subtract it from the original amount.

Exercise 5.3 A

1 Express the following as percentages. Round your answers to one decimal place.

(a) $\frac{1}{2}$ (b) $\frac{2}{3}$ (c) $\frac{1}{6}$ (d) $\frac{5}{8}$ (e) $\frac{93}{312}$

(f) 0.3 (g) 0.04 (h) 0.47 (i) 1.12 (j) 2.07

2 Express the following percentages as common fractions in their simplest form.

(a) 25% (b) 80% (c) 90% (d) 12.5%

(e) 50% (f) 98% (g) 60% (h) 22%

3 Calculate.

(a) 30% of 200 kg (b) 40% of $60 (c) 25% of 600 litres (d) 22% of 250 ml

(e) 50% of $128 (f) 65% of £30 (g) 15% of 120 km (h) 0.5% of 40 grams

(i) 2.6% of $80 (j) 9.5% of 5000 m³ (k) 2.5% of $80 (l) 120% of 3.5kg

> **Tip**
> When finding a percentage of a quantity, your answer will have a unit and not a percentage sign because you are working out an amount.

4 Calculate the percentage increase or decrease and copy and complete the table. Round your answers to one decimal place.

	Original amount	New amount	Percentage increase or decrease
(a)	40	48	
(b)	4000	3600	
(c)	1.5	2.3	
(d)	12 000	12 400	
(e)	12 000	8600	
(f)	9.6	12.8	
(g)	90	2400	

5 Increase each amount by the given percentage.

(a) $48 increased by 14% (b) $700 increased by 35%

(c) $30 increased by 7.6% (d) $40 000 increased by 0.59%

(e) $90 increased by 9.5% (f) $80 increased by 24.6%

6 Decrease each amount by the given percentage.

    (a) $68 decreased by 14%   (b) $800 decreased by 35%

    (c) $90 decreased by 7.6%   (d) $20 000 decreased by 0.59%

    (e) $85 decreased by 9.5%   (f) $60 decreased by 24.6%

Exercise 5.3 B

1 75 250 tickets were available for an international cricket match. 62% of the tickets were sold within a day. How many tickets are left?

2 Mrs Rajah owns 15% of a company. If the company issues 12 000 shares, how many shares should she get?

3 A building, which cost $125 000 to build, increased in value by $3\frac{1}{2}$ %. What is the building worth now?

4 A player scored 18 out of the 82 points in a basketball match. What percentage of the points did he score?

5 A company has a budget of $24 000 for printing brochures. The marketing department has spent 34.6% of the budget already. How much money is left in the budget?

6 Josh currently earns $6000 per month. If he receives an increase of 3.8%, what will his new monthly earnings be?

7 A company advertises that its cottage cheese is 99.5% fat free. If this is correct, how many grams of fat would there be in a 500 gram tub of the cottage cheese?

8 Sally earns $25 per shift. Her boss says she can either have $7 more per shift or a 20% increase. Which is the better offer?

5.4 Standard form

- A number in standard form is written as: a number ≥ 1 but < 10 multiplied by 10 raised to a power.
- Standard form is also called scientific notation.
- To write a number in standard form:
  - first, place a decimal point after the first significant digit
  - then, count the number of place orders the first significant digits has to move to get from this new number to the original number, this gives the power of 10
  - finally, if the significant digit has moved to the left from the new number to get to the original (note this *looks* like the decimal point has moved to the right), has moved to the 10, the power of 10 is positive, but if the significant digit has moved to the right (or decimal to the left), the power of 10 is negative.
- To write a number in standard form as an ordinary number, multiply the decimal fraction by 10 to the given power.

Tip

Make sure you know how your calculator deals with standard form.

Exercise 5.4 A

1 Write the following numbers in standard form.

    (a) 45 000   (b) 800 000   (c) 80   (d) 2 345 000

    (e) 4 190 000   (f) 32 000 000 000   (g) 0.0065   (h) 0.009

    (i) 0.00045   (j) 0.0000008   (k) 0.00675   (l) 0.00000000045

If the number part of your standard form answer is a whole number, there is no need to add a decimal point.

2 Write the following as ordinary numbers.

(a) 2.5×10^3 (b) 3.9×10^4 (c) 4.265×10^5 (d) 1.045×10^{-5}

(e) 9.15×10^{-6} (f) 1×10^{-9} (g) 2.8×10^{-5} (h) 9.4×10^7

(i) 2.45×10^{-3}

REWIND

Remember, the first significant figure is the first non-zero digit from the left. ◄

Exercise 5.4 B

1 Calculate, giving your answers in standard form correct to three significant figures.

(a) 4216^6 (b) $(0.00009)^4$ (c) $0.0002 \div 2500^3$

(d) $65\,000\,000 \div 0.0000045$ (e) $(0.0029)^3 \times (0.00365)^5$ (f) $(48 \times 987)^4$

(g) $\dfrac{4525 \times 8760}{0.00002}$ (h) $\dfrac{9500}{0.0005^4}$ (i) $\sqrt{5.25} \times 10^8$

2 Simplify each of the following. Give your answer in standard form.

(a) $(3 \times 10^{12}) \times (4 \times 10^{18})$ (b) $(1.5 \times 10^6) \times (3 \times 10^5)$ (c) $(1.5 \times 10^{12})^3$

(d) $(1.2 \times 10^{-5}) \times (1.1 \times 10^{-6})$ (e) $(0.4 \times 10^{15}) \times (0.5 \times 10^{12})$ (f) $(8 \times 10^{17}) \div (3 \times 10^{12})$

(g) $(1.44 \times 10^8) \div (1.2 \times 10^6)$ (h) $(8 \times 10^{-15}) \div (4 \times 10^{-12})$ (i) $\sqrt[3]{9.1} \times 10^{-8}$

3 The Sun has a mass of approximately 1.998×10^{27} tonnes. The planet Mercury has a mass of approximately 3.302×10^{20} tonnes.

(a) Which has the greater mass?

(b) How many times heavier is the greater mass compared with the smaller mass?

4 Light travels at a speed of 3×10^8 metres per second. The Earth is an average distance of 1.5×10^{11} m from the Sun and Pluto is an average 5.9×10^{12} m from the Sun.

(a) Work out how long it takes light from the Sun to reach Earth (in seconds). Give your answer in both ordinary numbers and standard form.

(b) How much longer does it take for the light to reach Pluto? Give your answer in both ordinary numbers and standard form.

5.5 Estimation

- Estimating involves rounding values in a calculation to numbers that are easy to work with (usually without the need for a calculator).
- An estimate allows you to check that your calculations make sense.

Exercise 5.5

Remember, the symbol ≈ means 'is approximately equal to'.

1 Use whole numbers to show why these estimates are correct.

(a) $3.9 \times 5.1 \approx 20$ (b) $68 \times 5.03 \approx 350$

(c) $999 \times 6.9 \approx 7000$ (d) $42.02 \div 5.96 \approx 7$

2 Estimate the answers to each of these calculations to the nearest whole number.

(a) $5.2 + 16.9 - 8.9 + 7.1$ (b) $(23.86 + 9.07) \div (15.99 - 4.59)$

(c) $\dfrac{9.3 \times 7.6}{5.9 \times 0.95}$ (d) $8.9^2 \times \sqrt{8.98}$

Mixed exercise

1 Estimate the answer to each of these calculations to the nearest whole number.

    (a) 9.75×4.108 **(b)** $0.0387 \div 0.00732$ **(c)** $\dfrac{36.4 \times 6.32}{9.987}$ **(d)** $\sqrt{64.25} \times 3.098^2$

2 Simplify.

    (a) $\dfrac{160}{200}$ **(b)** $\dfrac{48}{72}$ **(c)** $\dfrac{36}{54}$

3 Calculate.

    (a) $\dfrac{4}{9} \times \dfrac{3}{8}$ **(b)** $84 \times \dfrac{3}{4}$ **(c)** $\dfrac{5}{9} \div \dfrac{1}{3}$ **(d)** $\dfrac{4}{15} + \dfrac{9}{15}$ **(e)** $\dfrac{9}{11} - \dfrac{3}{4}$

    (f) $\dfrac{5}{24} + \dfrac{7}{16}$ **(g)** $2\dfrac{1}{3} + 9\dfrac{1}{2}$ **(h)** $\left(4\dfrac{3}{4}\right)^2$ **(i)** $9\dfrac{1}{5} - 1\dfrac{7}{9}$

4 A family spends $\dfrac{1}{3}$ of their income on insurance and medical expenses, $\dfrac{1}{4}$ on living expenses and $\dfrac{1}{6}$ on savings. What fraction is left over?

5 Express the first quantity as a percentage of the second.

    (a) $400, $5000   **(b)** 4.8, 96   **(c)** 19, 30

6 A traffic officer pulls over 12 drivers at random from 450 passing cars. What percentage of drivers is this?

7 Find:

    (a) 30% of 82 kg   **(b)** 2.5% of 20 litres   **(c)** 17.5% of $400.

8 Express the following as percentages.

    (a) $\dfrac{1}{8}$ **(b)** $\dfrac{1}{3}$ **(c)** 425 out of 1250

9 Increase $90 by 15%.

10 Decrease $42.50 by 12%.

11 A baby weighed 3.25 kg when she was born. After 12 weeks, her mass had increased to 5.45 kg. Express this as a percentage increase, correct to one decimal place.

12 An aeroplane was flying at a height of 10 500 m when one engine failed. The plane dropped 28% in height. How many metres did it drop?

13 Joshua is paid $20.45 per hour. He normally works a 38-hour week.

    (a) Estimate his weekly earnings to the nearest dollar.
    (b) Estimate his annual earnings.

14 Pluto is 5.9×10^{12} m from the Sun.

    (a) Express this in kilometres, giving your answer in standard form.
    (b) In a certain position, the Earth is 1.47×10^8 km from the Sun. If Pluto, the Earth and the Sun are in a straight line in this position (and both planets are the same side of the Sun), calculate the approximate distance, in km, between the Earth and Pluto. Give your answer in standard form.

6 Equations and transforming formulae

6.1 Further expansions of brackets

- Expand means to remove the brackets by multiplying out.
- Each term inside the bracket must be multiplied by the term outside the bracket.
- Negative terms in front of the brackets will affect the signs of the expanded terms.

Remember:

$+ \times - = -$

$- \times + = -$

$+ \times + = +$

$- + - = +$

Exercise 6.1

1 Expand and simplify if possible.

(a) $-2(x+y)$ (b) $-5(a-b)$ (c) $-3(-2x+y)$

(d) $2x(4-2y)$ (e) $-2x(x+3y)$ (f) $-9(x-1)$

(g) $3(4-2a)$ (h) $3-(4x+y)$ (i) $2x-(2x-3)$

(j) $-(3x+7)$ (k) $2x(x-y)$ (l) $-3x(x-2y)$

2 Expand and simplify as far as possible.

(a) $2(x-y)+3x(4-3)$ (b) $-4x(y-3)-(2x+xy)$ (c) $-2(x+3y)-2x(y-4)$

(d) $-\frac{1}{2}x(4-2y)-2y(3+x)$ (e) $12xy-(2+y)-3(4-x)$ (f) $2x^2(2-2y)-y(3-2x^2)$

(g) $-\frac{1}{4}x(4x-8)+2-(x^2-3)$ (h) $-2(x^2-2y)+4x(2x-2y)$ (i) $-\frac{1}{2}(8x-2)+3-(x+7)$

6.2 Solving linear equations

- To solve an equation, you find the value of the unknown letter (variable) that makes the equation true.
- If you add or subtract the same number (or term) to both sides of the equation, you produce an equivalent equation and the solution remains unchanged.
- If you multiply or divide each term on both sides of the equation by the same number (or term), you produce an equivalent equation and the solution remains unchanged.

Exercise 6.2

In this exercise leave answers as fractions rather than decimals, where necessary.

1 Solve these equations.

(a) $x+5=21$ (b) $x-10=14$ (c) $4x=32$ (d) $\frac{x}{6}=9$

(e) $9x=63$ (f) $x-2=-4$ (g) $x+7=-9$ (h) $\frac{x}{5}=-12$

(i) $x-4=-13$ (j) $-4x=60$ (k) $-2x=-26$ (l) $-3x=-45$

2 Solve these equations for x. Show the steps in your working.

(a) $2x+3=19$ (b) $3x-9=36$ (c) $2x+9=4$

(d) $4-2x=24$ (e) $-4x+5=21$ (f) $-2x-9=15$

The variable can appear on both sides of the equation. You can add or subtract variables to both sides just like numbers.

3 Solve these equations for x. Show the steps in your working.

(a) $2x+7=3x+4$ (b) $4x+6=x+18$ (c) $5x-2=3x+7$ (d) $9x-5=7x+3$

(e) $11x-4=x+32$ (f) $2x-1=14-x$ (g) $20-4x=5x+2$ (h) $3+4x=2x-7$

(i) $4x+5=7x-7$ (j) $2x-6=4x-3$ (k) $3x+2=5x-9$ (l) $x+9=5x-3$

4 Solve these equations for x.

When an equation has brackets it is usually best to expand them first.

(a) $3(x-2)=24$ (b) $5(x+4)=10$ (c) $3(3x+10)=6$ (d) $3(2x-1)=5$

(e) $-3(x-6)=-6$ (f) $4(3-5x)=7$ (g) $4(x+3)=x$ (h) $6(x+3)=4x$

(i) $3x+2=2(x-4)$ (j) $x-3=2(x+5)$ (k) $4(x+7)-3(x-5)=9$

(l) $2(x-1)-7(3x-2)=7(x-4)$

5 Solve these equations for x.

To remove the denominators of fractions in an equation, multiply each term on both sides by the common denominator.

(a) $\dfrac{x}{2}-3=6$ (b) $\dfrac{x}{3}+2=11$ (c) $\dfrac{4x}{6}=16$ (d) $\dfrac{28-x}{6}=12$

(e) $\dfrac{x-2}{3}=5$ (f) $\dfrac{x+3}{2}=16$ (g) $\dfrac{2x+5}{3}=9$ (h) $\dfrac{12x-1}{5}=9$

(i) $\dfrac{5x+2}{3}=-1$ (j) $\dfrac{5-2x}{4}=-1$ (k) $\dfrac{2x-1}{5}=x$ (l) $\dfrac{2x-3}{5}=x-6$

(m) $\dfrac{10x+2}{3}=6-x$ (n) $\dfrac{x}{2}-\dfrac{x}{5}=3$ (o) $\dfrac{2x}{3}-\dfrac{x}{2}=7$ (p) $-2\dfrac{(x+4)}{2}=x+7$

6.3 Factorising algebraic expressions

- The first step in factorising is to identify and 'take out' ALL common factors.
- Common factors can be numbers, variables, brackets or a combination of these.
- Factorising is the opposite of expanding – when you factorise you put brackets back into the expression.

Exercise 6.3

Remember, x^2 means $x \times x$, so x is a factor of x^2

1 Find the highest common factor of each pair.

(a) $3x$ and 21 (b) 40 and $8x$ (c) $15a$ and $5b$

(d) $2a$ and ab (e) $3xy$ and $12yz$ (f) $5a^2b$ and $20ab^2$

(g) $8xy$ and $28xyz$ (h) $9pq$ and p^2q^2 (i) $14abc$ and $7a^2b$

(j) x^2y^3z and $2xy^2z^2$ (k) $2a^2b^4$ and ab^3 (l) $3x^3y^2$ and $15xy$

Find the HCF of the numbers first. Then find the HCF of the variables, if there is one, in alphabetical order.

2 Factorise as fully as possible.

(a) $12x+48$ (b) $2+8y$ (c) $4a-16$ (d) $2x-12$

(e) $4x-20$ (f) $16a-8$ (g) $3x-xy$ (h) $ab+5a$

(i) $3x-15y$ (j) $8a+24$ (k) $12x-18$ (l) $24xyz-8xz$

(m) $9ab-12bc$ (n) $6xy-4yz$ (o) $14x-26xy$ (p) $-14x^2-7x^5$

Exercise 7.3

(Use π = 3.14 for any shapes involving circles in this exercise.)

1 Calculate the surface area of each shape.

(a)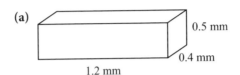

(b)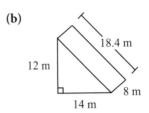

(c)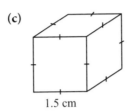

(d)

2 A wooden cube has six identical square faces, each of area 64 cm².

   (a) What is the surface area of the cube?

   (b) What is the height of the cube?

3 Mrs Nini is ordering wooden blocks to use in her maths classroom.
The blocks are cuboids with dimensions 10 cm × 8 cm × 5 cm.

   (a) Calculate the surface area of one block.

   (b) Mrs Nini needs 450 blocks. What is the total surface area of all the blocks?

   (c) She decides to varnish the blocks. A tin of varnish covers an area of 4 m².
How many tins will she need to varnish all the blocks?

4 Calculate the volume of each prism.

(a)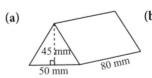

(b)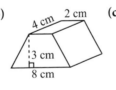

(c)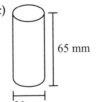

(d)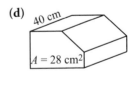

(e)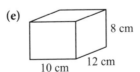

(f)

(g)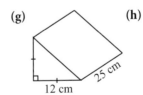

(h)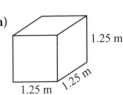

5 A pocket dictionary is 14 cm long, 9.5 cm wide and 2.5 cm thick.
Calculate the volume of space it takes up.

6 (a) Find the volume of a lecture room that is 8 m long, 8 m wide and 3.5 m high.

(b) Safety regulations state that during an hour long lecture each person in the room must have 5 m³ of air. Calculate the maximum number of people who can attend an hour long lecture.

7 A cylindrical tank is 30 m high with an inner radius of 150 cm. Calculate how much water the tank will hold when full.

8 A machine shop has four different rectangular prisms of volume 64 000 mm³. Copy and fill in the possible dimensions for each prism to complete the table.

Volume (mm³)	64 000	64 000	64 000	64 000
Length (mm)	80	50		
Breadth (mm)	40		80	
Height (mm)				16

Mixed exercise

1 A circular plate on a stove has a diameter of 21 cm. There is a metal strip around the outside of the plate.

(a) Calculate the surface area of the top of the plate.
(b) Calculate the length of the metal strip.

2 What is the radius of a circle with an area of 65 cm²?

3 Calculate the shaded area in each figure.

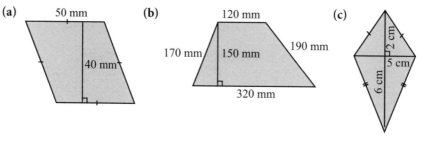

(a) 50 mm, 40 mm
(b) 120 mm, 170 mm, 150 mm, 190 mm, 320 mm
(c) 2 cm, 5 cm, 6 cm

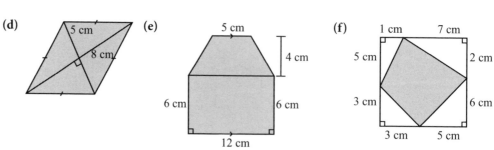

(d) 5 cm, 8 cm
(e) 5 cm, 4 cm, 6 cm, 6 cm, 12 cm
(f) 1 cm, 7 cm, 5 cm, 2 cm, 3 cm, 6 cm, 3 cm, 5 cm

4 *MNOP* is a trapezium with an area of 150 cm². Calculate the length of *NO*.

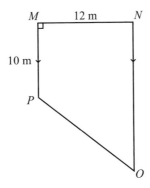

5 Study the two prisms.

(a)
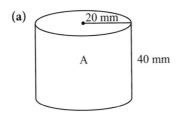

(b)
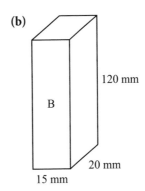

(a) Which of the two prisms has the smaller volume?

(b) What is the difference in volume?

(c) Sketch a net of the cuboid. Your net does not need to be to scale, but you must indicate the dimensions of each face on the net.

(d) Calculate the surface area of each prism.

6 How many cubes of side 4 cm can be packed into a wooden box measuring 32 cm by 16 cm by 8 cm?

Introduction to probability

8.1 Basic probability

- Probability is a measure of the chance that something will happen. It is measured on a scale of 0 to 1:
  - outcomes with a probability of 0 are impossible
  - outcomes with a probability of 1 are certain
  - an outcome with a probability of 0.5 or $\frac{1}{2}$ has an even chance of occurring.
- Probabilities can be found through doing an experiment, such as tossing a coin. Each time you perform the experiment is called a trial. If you want to get heads, then heads is your desired outcome or successful outcome.
- To calculate probability from the outcomes of experiments, use the formula:

$$\text{Experimental probability of outcome} = \frac{\text{number of successful outcomes}}{\text{number of trials}}$$

- Experimental probability is also called the relative frequency.

Exercise 8.1

> P(A), P(B), etc., are often used to express the probability of outcome A, B, etc. For example, the experimental probability of getting a six when you roll a die would be expressed as P(6).

1 Salma has a bag containing one red, one white and one green ball. She draws a ball at random and replaces it before drawing again. She repeats this 50 times. She uses a tally table to record the outcomes of her experiment.

Red	ЦНТ ЦНТ ЦНТ
White	ЦНТ ЦНТ ЦНТ |||
Green	ЦНТ ЦНТ ЦНТ ||

(a) Calculate the relative frequency of drawing each colour.
(b) Express her chance of drawing a red ball as a percentage.
(c) What is the sum of the three relative frequencies?
(d) What should your chances be in theory of drawing each colour?

2 It is Josh's job to call customers who have had their car serviced at the dealer to check whether they are happy with the service they received. He kept this record of what happened for 200 calls made one month.

Result	Frequency
Spoke to customer	122
Phone not answered	44
Left message on answering machine	22
Phone engaged or out of order	10
Wrong number	2

(a) Calculate the relative frequency of each event as a decimal fraction.

(b) Is it highly likely, likely, unlikely or highly unlikely that the following outcomes will occur when Josh makes a call:

(i)   the call will be answered by the customer

(ii) the call will be answered by a machine

(iii) he will dial the wrong number

8.2 Theoretical probability

- You can calculate the theoretical probability of an event without doing experiments if the outcomes are equally likely. Use the formula:

$$P(\text{outcome}) = \frac{\text{number of favourable outcomes}}{\text{number of possible outcomes}}$$

  For example, when you toss a coin you can get heads or tails (two possible outcomes). The probability of heads is $P(H) = \frac{1}{2}$.

- You need to work out what *all* the possible outcomes are before you can calculate theoretical probability.

Tip

It is helpful to list the possible outcomes so that you know what to substitute in the formula.

Remember, 1 is NOT a prime number.

Exercise 8.2

1 A container has three red and three blue counters in it. A counter is drawn and its colour is noted.

(a) What are the possible outcomes?

(b) What is the probability of drawing a red counter?

(c) Is it equally likely that you will draw red as blue?

2 An unbiased six-sided die with the numbers one to six on the faces is rolled.

(a) What are the possible outcomes of this event?

(b) Calculate the probability of rolling a prime number.

(c) What is the probability of rolling an even number?

(d) What is the probability of rolling a number greater than seven?

3 Sally has ten identical cards numbered one to ten. She draws a card at random and records the number on it.

(a) What are the possible outcomes for this event?

(b) Calculate the probability that Sally will draw:

(i)   the number five

(ii)   any one of the ten numbers

(iii) a multiple of three

(iv)   a number < 4

(v)   a number < 5

(vi)   a number < 6

(vii) a square number

(viii) a number < 10

(ix)   a number > 10

4 There are five cups of coffee on a tray. Two of them contain sugar.

(a) What are your chances of choosing a cup with sugar in it?

(b) Which choice is most likely? Why?

5 Mike has four cards numbered one to four. He draws one card and records the number. Calculate the probability that the result will be:

(a) a multiple of three   (b) a multiple of two   (c) factor of three

6 For a fly-fishing competition, the organisers place 45 trout, 30 salmon and 15 pike in a small dam.

(a) What is an angler's chance of catching a salmon on her first attempt?

(b) What is the probability she catches a trout?

(c) If the dam already contained same salmon and trout such that the probability of catching one of each was $\frac{8}{21}$ and $\frac{10}{21}$ respectively. What is the probability of catching a pike if there are still only 15 in the dam?

7 A dartboard is divided into 20 sectors numbered from one to 20. If a dart is equally likely to land in any of these sectors, calculate:

(a) P(<8)   (b) P(odd)   (c) P(prime)

(d) P(multiple of 3)   (e) P(multiple of 5).

8 A school has forty classrooms numbered from one to 40. Work out the probability that a classroom number has the numeral '1' in it.

8.3   The probability that an event does not happen

- An event may happen or it may not happen. For example, you may throw a six when you roll a die, but you may not.
- The probability of an event happening may be different from the probability of the event not happening, but the two combined probabilities will always add up to one.
- If A is an event happening, then A′ (or $\overline{A}$) represents the event A not happening and P(A′)=1 – P(A).

Exercise 8.3

1 The probability that a driver is speeding on a stretch of road is 0.27. What is the probability that a driver is not speeding?

2 The probability of drawing a green ball in an experiment is $\frac{3}{8}$. What is the probability of not drawing a green ball?

3 A container holds 300 sweets in five different flavours. The probability of choosing a particular flavour is given in the table.

Flavour	Strawberry	Lime	Lemon	Blackberry	Apple
P(flavour)	0.21	0.22	0.18	0.23	

(a) Calculate P(apple).

(b) What is P(not apple)?

(c) Calculate the probability of choosing P(neither lemon nor lime)?

(d) Calculate the number of each flavoured sweet in the packet.

4 In an opinion poll, 5000 teenagers were asked what make of mobile phone they would choose from four options (A, B, C or D). The probability of choosing each option is given in the table.

Phone	A	B	C	D
P(option)	0.36	0.12	0.4	

(a) Calculate P(D).

(b) What is P(D$'$)?

(c) What is the probability a teenager would choose either B or D?

(d) How many teenagers would you expect to choose option C if these probabilities are correct?

Mixed exercise

1 A coin is tossed a number of times giving the following results.

Heads: 4083   Tails: 5917

(a) How many times was the coin tossed?

(b) Calculate the relative frequency of each outcome.

(c) What is the probability that the next toss will result in heads?

(d) Jess says she thinks the results show that the coin is biased. Do you agree? Give a reason for your answer.

2 A bag contains 10 red, eight green and two white counters. Each counter has an equal chance of being chosen. Calculate the probability of:

(a) choosing a red ball

(b) choosing a green ball

(c) choosing a white ball

(d) choosing a blue ball

(e) choosing a red or a green ball

(f) not choosing a white ball

(g) choosing a ball that is not red

Sequences and sets

9.1 Sequences

- A number sequence is a list of numbers that follows a set pattern. Each number in the sequence is called a term. T_1 is the first term, T_{10} is the tenth term and T_n is the nth term, or general term.
- A linear sequence has a constant difference (d) between the terms. The general rule for finding the nth term of any linear sequence is $T_n = a + (n-1)d$, where a is the first value in the sequence.
- When you know the rule for making a sequence, you can find the value of any term. Substitute the term number into the rule and solve it.

You should recognise these sequences of numbers:
square numbers: 1, 4, 9, 16 . . .
cube numbers: 1, 8, 27, 64 . . .
triangular numbers: 1, 3, 6, 10 . . .
Fibonacci numbers: 1, 1, 2, 3, 5, 8 . . .

Exercise 9.1

1 Find the next three terms in each sequence and describe the rule you used to find them.

    (a) 11, 13, 15 . . .   **(b)** 88, 99, 110 . . .   **(c)** 64, 32, 16 . . .   **(d)** 8, 16, 24, 32 . . .
    (e) $-2, -4, -6, -8$ . . . **(f)** $\frac{1}{4}, \frac{1}{2}, 1$ . . .   **(g)** 1, 2, 4, 7 . . .   **(h)** 1, 6, 11, 16 . . .

2 List the first four terms of the sequences that follow these rules.

    (a) Start with seven and add two each time.
    (b) Start with 37 and subtract five each time.
    (c) Start with one and multiply by $\frac{1}{2}$ each time.
    (d) Start with five then multiply by two and add one each time.
    (e) Start with 100, divide by two and subtract three each time.

3 Write down the first three terms of each of these sequences. Then find the 35th term.

    (a) $T_n = 2n + 3$
    (b) $T_n = n^2$
    (c) $T_n = 6n - 1$
    (d) $T_n = n^3 - 1$
    (e) $T_n = n^2 - n$
    (f) $T_n = 3 - 2n$

4 Consider the sequence:

    2, 10, 18, 26, 34, 42, 50 . . .

    (a) Find the nth term of the sequence.
    (b) Find the 200th term.
    (c) Which term of this sequence has the value 234? Show full working.
    (d) Show that 139 is not a term in the sequence.

5 For each sequence below find the general term and the 50th term.

(a) 7, 9, 11, 13 . . .
(b) −5, − 13, − 21, − 29 . . .
(c) 2, 8, 14, 20, 26 . . .
(d) 4, 9, 16, 25 . . .
(e) 2.3, 3.5, 4.7, 5.9 . . .

9.2 Rational and irrational numbers

- You can express any rational number as a fraction in the form of $\frac{a}{b}$ where a and b are integers and $b \neq 0$.
- Whole numbers, integers, common fractions, mixed numbers, terminating decimal fractions and recurring decimals are all rational.
- You can convert recurring decimal fractions into the form $\frac{a}{b}$.
- Irrational numbers cannot be written in the form $\frac{a}{b}$. Irrational numbers are all non-recurring, non-terminating decimals.
- The set of real numbers is made up of rational and irrational numbers.

In $1.\dot{2}$, the dot above the two in the decimal part means it is recurring (the '2' repeats forever). If a set of numbers recurs, e.g. 0.273273273..., there will be a dot at the start and end of the recurring set: $0.\dot{2}7\dot{3}$.

Exercise 9.2

1 Write down all the irrational numbers in each set of real numbers.

(a) $\frac{3}{8}$, $\sqrt{16}$, $\sqrt[3]{16}$, $\frac{22}{7}$, $\sqrt{12}$, 0.090090009..., $\frac{31}{3}$, 0.020202...,

(b) 23, $\sqrt{45}$, $0.\dot{6}$, $\frac{3}{4}$, $\sqrt[3]{90}$, π, $5\frac{1}{2}$, $\sqrt{8}$, 0.834,

2 Convert each of the following recurring decimals to a fraction in its simplest form.

(a) $0.\dot{4}$ (b) $0.\dot{5}$ (c) $0.\dot{7}$
(d) $0.7\dot{4}$ (e) $0.4\dot{5}$ (f) $0.\dot{2}\dot{1}$

Mixed exercise

1 For each of the following sequences, find the nth term and the 120th term.

(a) 1, 6, 11, 16 . . .
(b) 20, 14, 8, 2 . . .
(c) 2, 5, 8, 11 . . .

2 Which of the following numbers are irrational?

$1\frac{5}{8}$, 0.213231234..., $\sqrt{25}$, $\frac{7}{17}$, 0.1, − 0.654, $\sqrt{2}$, $\frac{22}{5}$, 4π

3 Write each recurring decimal as a fraction in its simplest form.

(a) $0.\dot{2}$ (b) $0.4\dot{2}$ (c) $0.\dot{2}\dot{3}$ (d) $0.28\dot{6}$

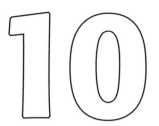

10 Straight lines and quadratic equations

10.1 Straight lines

- The position of a point can be uniquely described on the Cartesian plane using ordered pairs (x, y) of coordinates.
- You can use equations in terms of x and y to generate a table of paired values for x and y. You can plot these on the Cartesian plane and join them to draw a graph. To find y-values in a table of values, substitute the given (or chosen) x-values into the equation and solve for y.
- The gradient of a line describes its slope or steepness. Gradient can be defined as:

$$m = \frac{\text{change in } y}{\text{change in } x}$$

  - lines that slope up to the right have a positive gradient
  - lines that slope down to the right have a negative gradient
  - lines parallel to the x-axis (horizontal lines) have a gradient of 0
  - lines parallel to the y-axis (vertical lines) have an undefined gradient
  - lines parallel to each other have the same gradients.

- The equation of a straight line can be written in general terms as $y = mx + c$, where x and y are coordinates of points on the line, m is the gradient of the line and c is the y-intercept (the point where the graph crosses the y-axis).
- To find the equation of a given line you need to find the y-intercept and substitute this for c. Then you need to find the gradient of the line and substitute this for m.

Tip

Normally the x-values will be given. If not, choose three small values (for example, −2, 0 and 2). You need a minimum of three points to draw a graph. All graphs should be clearly labelled with their equation.

Remember, parallel lines have the same gradient.

Exercise 10.1

1 For x-values of −1, 0, 1, 2 and 3, draw a table of values for each of the following equations.

   (a) $y = x + 5$ (b) $y = -2x - 1$ (c) $y = 7 - 2x$ (d) $y = -x - 2$

   (e) $x = 4$ (f) $y = -2$ (g) $y = -2x - \frac{1}{2}$ (h) $4 = 2x - 5y$

   (i) $0 = x - 2y - 1$ (j) $x + y = -\frac{1}{2}$

2 Draw and label graphs (a) to (e) in question 1 on one set of axes and graphs (f) to (j) on another.

3 Find the equation of a line parallel to graph (a) in question 1 and passing through point (0, −2).

4 Are the following pairs of lines parallel or not?

   (a) $y = 3x + 3$ and $y = x + 3$ (b) $y = \frac{1}{2}x - 4$ and $y = \frac{1}{2}x - 8$

   (c) $y = -3x$ and $y = -3x + 7$ (d) $y = 0.8x - 7$ and $y = 8x + 2$

   (e) $2y = -3x + 2$ and $y = \frac{3}{2}x + 2$ (f) $2y - 3x = 2$ and $y = -1.5x + 2$

   (g) $y = 8$ and $y = -9$ (h) $x = -3$ and $x = \frac{1}{2}$

5 Find the gradient of the following lines.

(a)
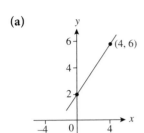

(b)
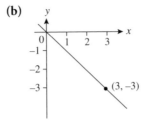

(c)
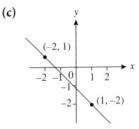

(d)
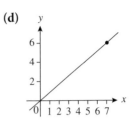

(e)
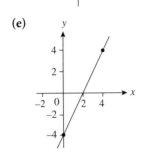

(f)
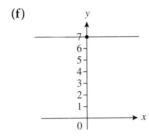

(g)
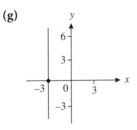

(h)
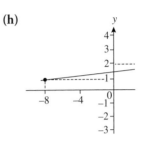

> **! Tip**
> You may need to rewrite the equations in the form $y = mx + c$ before you can do this.

6 Determine the gradient (m) and the y-intercept (c) of each of the following graphs.

(a) $y = 3x - 4$ (b) $y = -x - 1$ (c) $y = -\frac{1}{2}x + 5$ (d) $y = x$

(e) $y = \frac{x}{2} + \frac{1}{4}$ (f) $y = \frac{4x}{5} - 2$ (g) $y = 7$ (h) $y = -3x$

(i) $x + 3y = 14$ (j) $x + y + 4 = 0$ (k) $x - 4 = y$ (l) $2x = 5 - y$

(m) $x + \frac{y}{2} = -10$

7 Determine the equation of each of the following graphs.

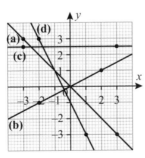

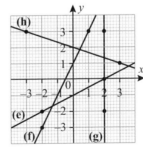

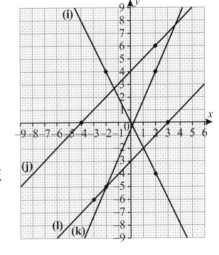

Mixed exercise

1 For each equation, copy and complete the table of values. Draw the graphs for all four equations on the same set of axes.

(a) $y = \frac{1}{2}x$

x	−1	0	2	3
y				

(b) $y = -\frac{1}{2}x + 3$

x	−1	0	2	3
y				

(c) $y = 2$

x	−1	0	2	3
y				

(d) $y - 2x - 4 = 0$

x	−1	0	2	3
y				

2 Determine the gradient and the y-intercept of each graph.

(a) $y = -2x - 1$ (b) $y + 6 = x$ (c) $x - y = -8$

(d) $y = -\frac{1}{2}$ (e) $2x + 3y = 6$ (f) $y = -x$

3 What equation defines each of these lines?

(a) a line with a gradient of 1 and a y-intercept of -3

(b) a line with a y-intercept of $\frac{1}{2}$ and a gradient of $-\frac{2}{3}$

(c) a line parallel to $y = -x + 8$ with a y-intercept of -2

(d) a line parallel to $y = -\frac{4}{5}x$ which passes through the point $(0, -3)$

(e) a line parallel to $2y - 4x + 2 = 0$ with a y-intercept of -3

(f) a line parallel to $x + y = 5$ which passes through $(1, 1)$

(g) a line parallel to the x-axis which passes through $(1, 2)$

(h) a line parallel to the y-axis which passes through $(-4, -5)$

4 Find the gradient of the following lines.

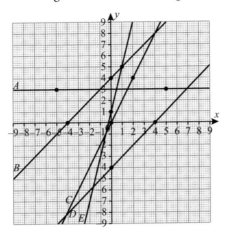

5 What is the equation of each of these lines?

(a)

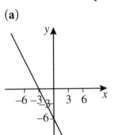

(b)

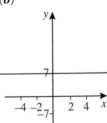

(c)

(d)

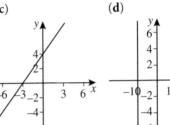

(e)

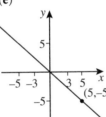

(f)

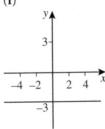

6 Caroline likes running. She averages a speed of 7 km/h when she runs. This relationship can be expressed as $D = 7t$, where D is the distance covered and t is the time (in hours) that she runs for.

(a) Use the formula $D = 7t$ to draw up a table of values for 0, 2, 4 and 6 hours of running.

(b) On a set of axes, draw a graph to show the relationship between D and t. Think carefully about how you will number the axes before you start.

(c) Write an equation in the form of $y = mx + c$ to describe this graph.

(d) What is the gradient of the line?

(e) Use your graph to find the time it takes Caroline to run:
   (i) 21 km   **(ii)** 10 km   **(iii)** 5 km.

(f) Use your graph to find out how far she runs in:
   (i) 3 hours   **(ii)** $2\frac{1}{2}$ hours   **(iii)** $\frac{3}{4}$ of an hour.

(g) Caroline enters the Two Oceans Marathon. The route is 42 km long, but it is very hilly. She estimates her average speed will drop to around 6 km/h. How long will it take her to complete the race if she runs at 6 km/h?

> **Tip**
>
> Time is usually plotted on the horizontal or x-axis because it is the independent variable in most relationships. In this graph you will only need to work in the first quadrant. You won't have any negative values because Caroline cannot run for less than 0 hours and her speed cannot be less than 0 km per hour.

11 Pythagoras' theorem and similar shapes

11.1 Pythagoras' theorem

- In a right-angled triangle, the square of the length of the hypotenuse (the longest side) is equal to the sum of the squares of the lengths of the other two sides. This can be expressed as $c^2 = a^2 + b^2$, where c is the hypotenuse and a and b are the two shorter sides of the triangle.
- Conversely, If $c^2 = a^2 + b^2$ then the triangle will be right-angled.
- To find the length of an unknown side in a right-angled triangle you need to know two of the sides. Then you can substitute the two known lengths into the formula and solve for the unknown length.

Exercise 11.1 A

Tip

The *hypotenuse* is the longest side. It is always opposite the right angle.

1 Calculate the length of the unknown side in each of these triangles.

(a)
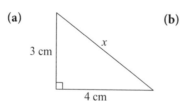
3 cm
x
4 cm

(b)
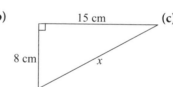
15 cm
8 cm
x

(c)
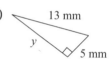
13 mm
y
5 mm

(d)
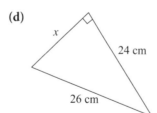
x
24 cm
26 cm

(e)
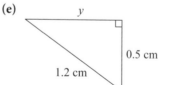
y
0.5 cm
1.2 cm

(f)
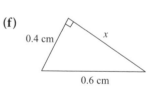
0.4 cm
x
0.6 cm

(g)
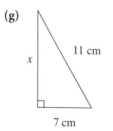
x
11 cm
7 cm

(h)
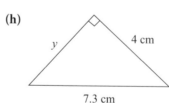
y
4 cm
7.3 cm

Mixed exercise

1   A school caretaker wants to mark out a sports field 50 m wide and 120 m long. To make sure that the field is rectangular, he needs to know how long each diagonal should be.

    (a) Draw a rough sketch of the field.

    (b) Calculate the required lengths of the diagonals.

2   In $\triangle ABC$, $AB = 10$ cm, $BC = 8$ cm and $AC = 6$ cm. Determine whether the triangle is right-angled or not and give reasons for your answer.

3   A triangle with sides of 25 mm, 65 mm and 60 mm is similar to another triangle with its longest side 975 mm. Calculate the perimeter of the larger triangle.

4   Calculate the missing dimensions in each of these pairs of similar triangles.

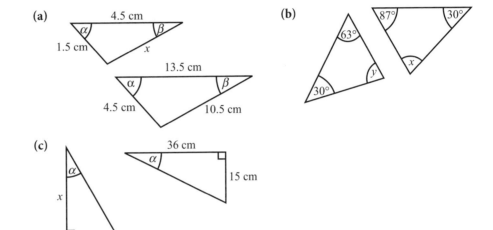

5   Two of the triangles in each set of three are congruent. State which two are congruent and give the conditions that you used to prove them congruent.

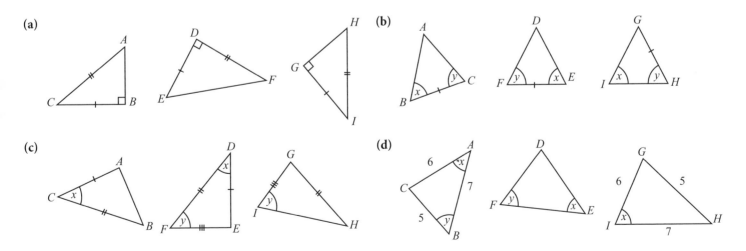

6 An 8.6 m long wire cable is used to secure a mast of height x m. The cable is attached to the top of the mast and secured on the ground 6.5 m away from the base of the mast. How tall is the mast? Give your answer correct to two decimal places.

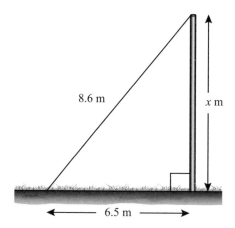

7 Nadia wants to have a metal number 1 made for her gate. She has found a sample brass numeral and noted its dimensions. She decides that her numeral should be similar to this one, but that it should be four times larger.

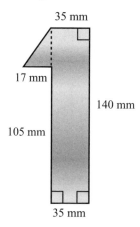

(a) Draw a rough sketch of the numeral that Nadia wants to make with the correct dimensions written on it in millimetres.

(b) Calculate the length of the sloping edge at the top of the full size numeral to the nearest whole millimetre.

12 Averages and measures of spread

12.1 Different types of average

- Statistical data can be summarised using an average (measure of central tendency) and a measure of spread (dispersion).
- There are three types of average: mean, median and mode.
- A measure of spread is the range (largest value minus smallest value).
- The mean is the sum of the data items divided by the number of items in the data set. The mean does not have to be one of the numbers in the data set.
  - The mean can be affected by extreme values in the data set. When one value is much lower or higher than the rest of the data it is called an outlier. Outliers skew the mean and make it less representative of the data set.
- The median is the middle value in a set of data when the data is arranged in increasing order.
  - When there is an even number of data items, the median is the mean of the two middle values.
- The mode is the number (or item) that appears most often in a data set.
  - When two numbers appear most often the data has two modes and is said to be bimodal. When more than two numbers appear equally often the mode has no real value as a statistic.

Exercise 12.1

1 Determine the mean, median and mode of the following sets of data.

  (a) 5, 9, 6, 4, 7, 6, 6
  (b) 23, 38, 15, 27, 18, 38, 21, 40, 27
  (c) 12, 13, 14, 12, 12, 13, 15, 16, 14, 13, 12, 11
  (d) 4, 4, 4, 5, 5, 5, 6, 6, 6
  (e) 4, 4, 4, 4, 5, 5, 6, 6, 6
  (f) 4, 4, 5, 5, 5, 6, 6, 6, 6

2 Five students scored a mean mark of 14.8 out of 20 for a maths test.

  (a) Which of these sets of marks fit this average?
    (i)   14, 16, 17, 15, 17   (ii) 12, 13, 12, 19, 19   (iii) 12, 19, 12, 18, 13
    (iv) 13, 17, 15, 16, 17   (v)   19, 19, 12, 0, 19   (vi) 15, 15, 15, 15, 14
  (b) Compare the sets of numbers in your answer above. Explain why you can get the same mean from different sets of numbers.

3 The mean of 15 numbers is 17. What is the sum of the numbers?

4 The sum of 21 numbers is 312.8. Which of the following numbers is closest to the mean of the 21 numbers? 14, 15, 16 or 17.

> **Tip**
> If you multiply the mean by the number of items in the data set, you get the total of the scores. This will help you solve problems like question 2.

5 An agricultural worker wants to know which of two dairy farmers have the best milk producing cows. Farmer Singh says his cows produce 2490 litres of milk per day. Farmer Naidoo says her cows produce 1890 litres of milk per day.

There is not enough information to decide which cows are the better producers of milk. What other information would you need to answer the question?

6 In a group of students, six had four siblings, seven had five siblings, eight had three siblings, nine had two siblings and ten had one sibling.

Siblings are brothers and sisters.

> **! Tip**
> It may help to draw up a rough frequency table to solve problems like this one.

(a) What is the total number students?
(b) What is the total number of siblings?
(c) What is the mean number of siblings?
(d) What is the modal number of siblings?

7 The management of a factory announced salary increases and said that workers would receive an average increase of $20 to $40.

The table shows the old and new salaries of the workers in the factory.

	Previous salary	Salary with increase
Four workers in Category A	$180	$240
Two workers in Category B	$170	$200
Six workers in Category C	$160	$170
Eight workers in Category D	$150	$156

(a) Calculate the mean increase for all workers.
(b) Calculate the modal increase.
(c) What is the median increase?
(d) How many workers received an increase of between $20 and $40?
(e) Was the management announcement true? Say why or why not.

12.2 Making comparisons using averages and ranges

- You can use averages to compare two or more sets of data. However, averages on their own may be misleading, so it is useful to work with other summary statistics as well.
- The range is a measure of how spread out (dispersed) the data is. Range = largest value – smallest value.
- A large range means that the data is spread out, so the measures of central tendency (averages) may not be representative of the whole data set.

> **! Tip**
> When the mean is affected by extreme values the median is more representative of the data.

Exercise 12.2

1 For the following sets of data, one of the three averages is not representative. State which one is not representative in each case.

(a) 6, 2, 5, 1, 5, 7, 2, 3, 8
(b) 2, 0, 1, 3, 1, 6, 2, 9, 10, 3, 2, 2, 0
(c) 21, 29, 30, 14, 5, 16, 3, 24, 17

15 Scale drawing, bearings and trigonometry

15.1 Scale drawings

- The scale of a diagram, or a map, can be given as a fraction or a ratio.
- A scale of $1:50\,000$ means that every line in the diagram has a length which is $\frac{1}{50000}$ of the length of the line that it represents in real life. For example 1 cm in the diagram represents $50\,000$ cm (or 0.5 km) in real life.

Exercise 15.1

◀ REWIND

Revise your metric conversions from chapter 13. ◀

1 (a) The basic pitch size of a rugby field is 100 m long and 70 m wide. A scale drawing of a field is made with a scale of 1 cm to 10 m. What is the length and width of the field in the drawing?

   (b) The pitch size, including the area inside the goal, is 144 m long and 70 m wide. What are these dimensions in the drawing of this pitch?

2 (a) The pitch size of a standard hockey field is 91.4 m long and 55 m wide. A scale drawing of a hockey field is made with a scale of $1:1000$. What are the dimensions of the hockey field in the drawing?

   (b) A school that wants to hold a Seven-A-Side hockey tournament has three standard hockey fields at their Sports Centre. Would it be possible to have five matches taking place at the same time, if the size of the pitch used for Seven-A-Side hockey is 55 m × 43 m?

A5 is half A4 and has dimensions 14.8 cm × 21 cm.

3 (a) The size of a tennis court is 23.77 m × 10.97 m. What would be a good scale for a drawing of a tennis court if you can only use half of an A4 page? Express this scale as a fraction.

   (b) (i) Make an accurate scale drawing, using your scale. Include all the markings as shown in the diagram below.

        (ii) The net posts are placed 1 m outside the doubles side lines. Mark each net post with an x on your scale drawing.

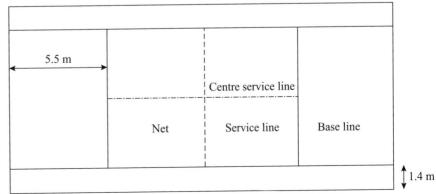

4 **(a)** The karate combat area measures $8\,m \times 8\,m$. Using a scale drawing and a scale of your choice, calculate the length of the diagonal.

(b) What would be a more accurate way to determine the length of the diagonal?

15.2 Bearings

- A bearing is a way of describing direction.
- Bearings are measured clockwise from the north direction.
- Bearings are always expressed using three figures.

Exercise 15.2

1 Give the three-figure bearing corresponding to:

(a) east   **(b)** south-west   **(c)** north-west.

2 Write down the three-figure bearings of X from Y.

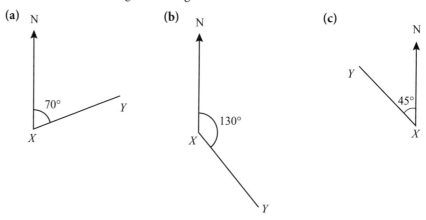

3 Village A is $7.5\,km$ east and $8\,km$ north of village B. Village C is $5\,km$ from village B on a bearing of $300°$. Using a scale drawing with a scale of $1:100\,000$ find:

(a) the bearing of village B from village A

(b) the bearing of village A from village C

(c) the direct distance between village B and village A

(d) the direct distance between village C and village A.

15.3 Understanding the tangent, cosine and sine ratios

- The hypotenuse is the longest side of a right-angled triangle.
- The opposite side is the side opposite a specified angle.
- The adjacent side is the side that forms a specified angle with the hypotenuse.
- The tangent ratio is $\dfrac{\text{the opposite side}}{\text{the adjacent side}}$ of a specified angle.
  - $\tan\theta = \dfrac{\text{opp}(\theta)}{\text{adj}(\theta)}$, $\quad$ $\text{opp}(\theta) = \text{adj}(\theta) \times \tan\theta$, $\quad$ $\text{adj}(\theta) = \dfrac{\text{opp}(\theta)}{\tan\theta}$
- The sine ratio is $\dfrac{\text{the opposite side}}{\text{the hypotenuse}}$ of a specified angle.
  - $\sin\theta = \dfrac{\text{opp}(\theta)}{\text{hyp}}$, $\quad$ $\text{opp}(\theta) = \text{hyp} \times \sin\theta$, $\quad$ $\text{hyp} = \dfrac{\text{opp}(\theta)}{\sin\theta}$
- The cosine ratio is $\dfrac{\text{the adjacent side}}{\text{the hypotenuse}}$ of a specified angle.
  - $\cos\theta = \dfrac{\text{adj}(\theta)}{\text{hyp}}$, $\quad$ $\text{adj}(\theta) = \text{hyp} \times \cos\theta$, $\quad$ $\text{hyp} = \dfrac{\text{adj}(\theta)}{\cos\theta}$

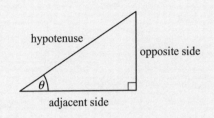

Exercise 15.3

1 Copy and complete the following table:

	(a)	(b)	(c)	(d)
	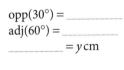			
hypotenuse				
opp(A)				
adj(A)				

2 Copy and complete the statement(s) alongside each triangle.

Remember, when working with right-angled triangles you may still need to use Pythagoras.

(a)

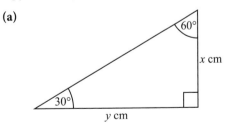

opp(30°) = ...
adj(60°) = ...
.... = y cm

(b)

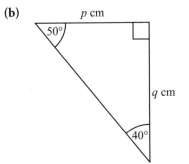

.... (40°) = q cm
.... (50°) = q cm
.... = p cm

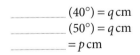

The memory aid, SOHCAHTOA, or the triangle diagrams

may help you remember the trigonometric relationships.

3 Calculate the value of the following tangent ratios, using your calculator. Give your answers to two decimal places where necessary.

(a) tan 33°

(b) tan 55°

(c) tan 79°

(d) tan 22.5°

(e) tan 0°

4 Copy and complete the statements for each of the following triangles, giving your answer as a fraction in its lowest terms where necessary:

(a)

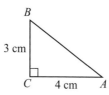

tan A =

(b)

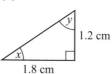

tan x =
tan y =

(c)

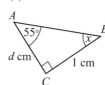

tan 55° =
x =
tan B =

(d)

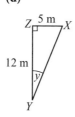

tan y =
∠X =
tan X =

(e)

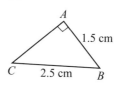

AC =
tan B =
tan C =

5 Calculate the unknown length (to two decimal places) in each case presented below.

(a)

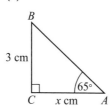

(b)

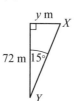

(c)

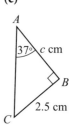

(d)

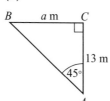

(e)

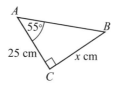

2 Use a graphical method to solve the following equations simultaneously.

(a) $y = 2x^2 + 3x - 2$ and $y = x + 2$

(b) $y = x^2 + 2x$ and $y = -x + 4$

(c) $y = -2x^2 + 2x + 4$ and $y = -2x - 4$

(d) $y = -0.5x^2 + x + 1.5$ and $y = \dfrac{1}{2}x$

Mixed exercise

1 (a) Copy and complete the tables below for the following equations, $y = x^2 - 8$ and $y = 2x - 3$. Then plot and draw the graphs of the equations onto the same pair of axes.

x	−3	−2	−1	0	1	2	3	4
$y = x^2 - 8$								

x	−1	−2	−1	0	1	2	3	4
$y = 2x - 3$								

(b) Using your graph, determine the value of x when $x^2 - 8 = 2x - 3$.

(c) What is the minimum value of $y = x^2 - 8$?

2 The dotted line on the grid below is the axis of symmetry for the given hyperbola.

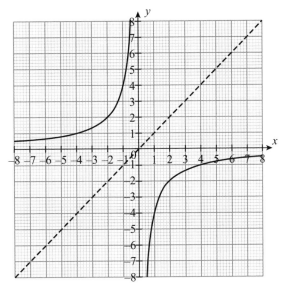

(a) Give the equation for the hyperbola.

(b) Give the equation for the given line of symmetry.

(c) Copy the diagram into your workbook and draw in the other line of symmetry, giving the equation for this line.

Symmetry and loci

19.1 Symmetry in two dimensions

- Two-dimensional (flat) shapes have line symmetry if you are able to draw a line through the shape so that one side of the line is the mirror image (reflection) of the other side. There may be more than one possible line of symmetry in a shape.

- If you rotate (turn) a shape around a fixed point and it fits on to itself during the rotation, then it has rotational symmetry. The number of times the shape fits on to its original position during a rotation is called the order of rotational symmetry.

If a shape can only fit back into itself after a full 360° rotation, it has no rotational symmetry.

Exercise 19.1

1 For each of the following shapes:

    (a) copy the shape and draw in any lines of symmetry

    (b) determine the order of rotational symmetry.

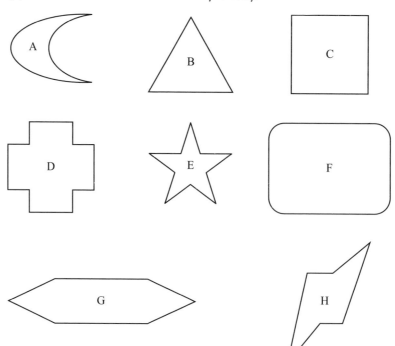

2 (a) How many lines of symmetry does a rhombus have? Draw a diagram to show your solution.

    (b) What is the order of rotational symmetry of a rhombus?

3 Draw a quadrilateral that has no lines of symmetry and no rotational symmetry.

19.2 Angle relationships in circles

- When a triangle is drawn in a semi-circle, so that one side is the diameter and the vertex opposite the diameter touches the circumference, the angle of the vertex opposite the diameter is a right angle (90°).
- Where a tangent touches a circle, the radius drawn to the same point meets the tangent at 90°.

Exercise 19.2

The angle relationships for triangles, quadrilaterals and parallel lines (chapter 3), as well as Pythagoras' theorem (chapter 11), may be needed to solve circle problems.

1 Given that O is the centre of the circle, calculate the value of $B\hat{A}D$ with reasons.

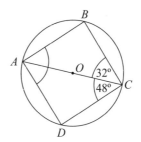

2 DC is a tangent to the circle with centre O. Find the size of $\angle DCA$.

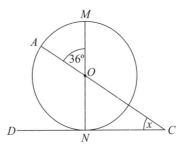

3 EC is a tangent to the circle with centre O. AB is a straight line and angle $CBD = 37°$. Calculate the size of the angles marked w, x, y and z giving reasons for each.

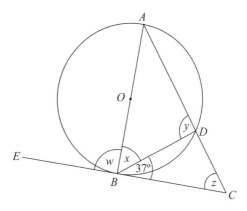

19.3 Locus

- A locus is a set of points that satisfy a given rule. A locus can be a straight line, a curve or a combination of straight and curved lines.
- The locus of points equidistant from a given point is a circle.
- The locus of points equidistant from a fixed line is two lines parallel to the given line.
- The locus of points equidistant from a given line segment is a 'running track' shape around the line segment.
- The locus of points equidistant from the arms of an angle is the bisector of the angle.
- To find the locus of points that are the same distance from two or more given points you have to use a combination of the loci above to find the intersections of the loci.

REWIND

Make sure you know to bisect an angle as this is often required in loci problems (see chapter 3). ◀

Exercise 19.3

1 Copy the diagrams and draw the locus of the points that are 3 cm from the point or lines in each case.

(a) • *A*   (b)    (c)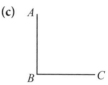

2 Construct a circle with centre *O* and a radius of 4 cm.

(a) Draw the locus of points that are 1 cm from the circumference of the circle.

(b) Shade the locus of points that are less than 1 cm from circumference of the circle.

3 In this scale diagram, the shaded area represents a fishpond. The fishpond is surrounded by a concrete walkway 2 m wide. Copy the diagram and draw the locus of points that are 2 m from the edges of the fishpond. Shade the area covered by the concrete walkway.

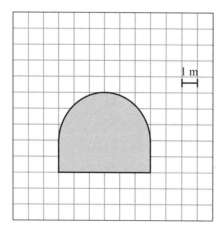

2 Make a copy of the diagram below and carry out the following transformations.

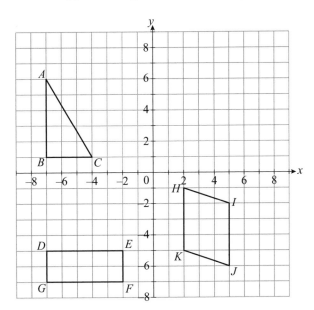

(a) Translate $\triangle ABC$ three units to the right and four units up. Label the image correctly.

(b) Reflect rectangle $DEFG$ about the line $y = -3$. Label the image correctly.

(c) (i) Rotate parallelogram $HIJK$ 90° anticlockwise about point $(2, -1)$.

   (ii) Translate the image $H'I'J'K'$ one unit left and five units up.

3 Make a copy of the diagram below and carry out the following transformations.

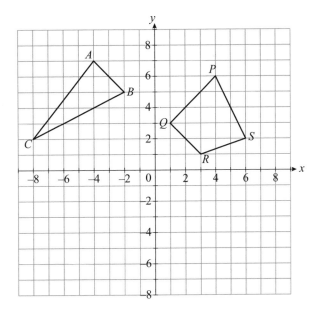

(a) $\triangle ABC$ is translated using the column vector $\begin{pmatrix} 10 \\ -9 \end{pmatrix}$ to form the image $A'B'C'$. Draw and label the image.

(b) Quadrilateral $PQRS$ is reflected in the y-axis and then translated using the column vector $\begin{pmatrix} 0 \\ 6 \end{pmatrix}$. Draw the resultant image $P'Q'R'S'$.

4 For each of the reflections shown in the diagram, give the equation of the mirror line.

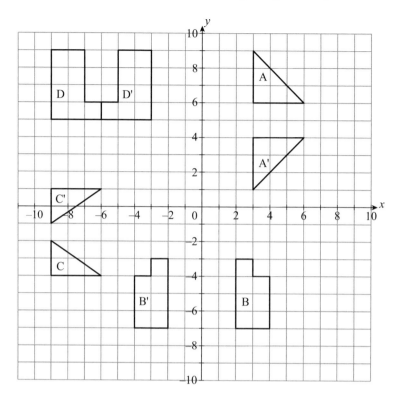

5 Copy the diagram for question 4 and draw the reflection of each shape (A–D) in the *x*-axis.

6 In each of the following, fully describe at least two different transformations that map the object onto its image.

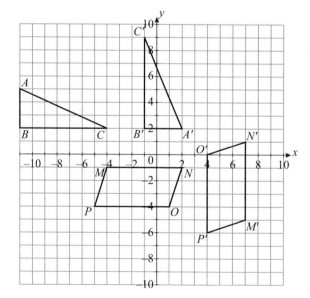

(g) $6x^2 + 2x$　　**(h)** $2x + 7$
(i) $4x + 18$　　**(j)** $15x - 6y$

6 **(a)** $9a + b$
　　(b) $x^2 + 3x - 2$
　　(c) $-4a^4b + 6a^2b^3$
　　(d) $-7x + 4$
　　(e) $\dfrac{4x}{y}$
　　(f) $5x - \dfrac{5y}{2}$

7 **(a)** $11x - 3$
　　(b) $6x^2 + 15x - 8$
　　(c) $-2x^2 + 5x + 12$
　　(d) $-x^3 + 3x^2 - x + 5$

8 **(a)** $\dfrac{5x^5}{6}$　　**(b)** 15
　　(c) $\dfrac{1}{x^4}$　　**(d)** $16x^4y^8$
　　(e) $\dfrac{64x^9}{y^{15}}$　　**(f)** x^9y^8
　　(g) $\dfrac{9x^4}{4y^3}$　　**(h)** $\dfrac{xy^6}{2}$

Chapter 3

Exercise 3.1 A

1 **(a)** obtuse, $112°$　　**(b)** acute, $32°$
　　(c) right, $90°$　　**(d)** reflex, $279°$
　　(e) obtuse, $125°$　　**(f)** reflex, $193°$

2 **(a)** **(i)** $90°$ **(ii)** $180°$
　　(b) $30°$
　　(c) $360°$
　　(d) quarter to one or 12:45

3 No. If the acute angle is $\leq 45°$ it will produce an acute or right angle.

4 Yes. The smallest obtuse angle is $91°$ and the largest is $179°$. Half of those will range from $45.5°$ to $89.5°$, all of which are acute.

5 **(a)** $45°$　　**(b)** $28°$
　　(c) $(90 - x)°$　　**(d)** $x°$

6 **(a)** $135°$　　**(b)** $90°$
　　(c) $76°$　　**(d)** $(180 - x)°$
　　(e) $x°$　　**(f)** $(90 + x)°$
　　(g) $(90 - x)°$　　**(h)** $220 - 2x$

Exercise 3.1 B

1 $z = 65°$ ($\angle$s on line); $y = 65°$ (VO); $x = 25$ (comp $\angle$ to z)

2 $\angle QON = 48°$, so $a = 48°$ (VO)

3 **(a)** $\angle EOD = 41°$ ($\angle$s on line), so $x = 41°$ (VO)
　　(b) $x = 20°$ ($\angle$s round point)

Exercise 3.1 C

1 $\angle HGB = 143°$ ($\angle$s on line); $\angle AGF = 143°$ (VO); $\angle BGF = 37°$ (VO); $\angle DFG = 143°$ (corr $\angle$s); $\angle CFG = 37°$ (corr $\angle$s); $\angle CFE = 143°$ (VO); $\angle EFD = 37°$ (VO)

2 **(a)** $x = 68°$ ($\angle BFG = 68°$, $\angle$s on line, then alt $\angle$s)
　　(b) $x = 85°$ (co-int $\angle$s); $y = 72°$ (alt $\angle$s)
　　(c) $x = 99°$ (co-int $\angle$s); $y = 123°$ ($\angle ABF = 123°$, co-int $\angle$s then VO)
　　(d) $x = 47°$ (alt $\angle$s); $y = 81°$ ($\angle$s in triangle BEF or on st line); $z = 52°$ (Alt $\angle$s)
　　(e) $x = 72°$ ($\angle BFE = 72°$, then alt $\angle$s); $y = 43°$ ($\angle$s in triangle BCJ)
　　(f) $x = 45°$ ($\angle$s round a point); $y = 90°$ (co-int $\angle$s)

3 **(a)** $x = 15°$ (co-int $\angle$s)
　　(b) $x = 60°$ (co-int $\angle$s)
　　(c) $x = 45°$ ($\angle STQ$ corr $\angle$s then VO)
　　(d) $x = 77.5°$ and $y = 75°$ (co-int $\angle$s)
　　(e) $x = 90°$ ($\angle ECD$ and $\angle ACD$ co-int $\angle$s then $\angle$s round as point)
　　(f) $x = 18°$ ($\angle DFE$ co-int with $\angle CDF$ then $\angle BFE$ co-int with $\angle ABF$)

Exercise 3.2

1 **(a)** $74°$ ($\angle$s in triangle)
　　(b) $103°$ ($\angle$s in triangle)
　　(c) $58°$ (ext $\angle$ equals sum int opps)
　　(d) $51°$ (ext $\angle$ equals sum int opps)
　　(e) $21°$ (ext $\angle$ equals sum int opps)
　　(f) $68°$ (ext $\angle$ equals sum int opps)
　　(g) $53°$ (base $\angle$s isosceles)
　　(h) $60°$ (equilateral triangle)

(i) $x = 58°$ (base $\angle$s isosceles and $\angle$s in triangle); $y = 26°$ (ext $\angle$s equals sum int opps)
(j) $x = 33°$ (base $\angle$s isosceles then ext $\angle$s equals sum int opps)
(k) $x = 45°$ (co-int $\angle$s then $\angle$s in triangle)
(l) $x = 45°$ (base $\angle$s isosceles); $y = 75°$ (base $\angle$s isosceles)

2 **(a)** $x = 36$; so $A = 36°$ and $B = 72°$
　　(b) $x = 40$; so $A = 80°$; $B = 40°$ and $\angle ACD = 120°$
　　(c) $x = 60°$
　　(d) $x = 72°$
　　(e) $x = 60$; so $R = 60°$ and $\angle RTS = 120°$
　　(f) $x = 110°$

Exercise 3.3

1 **(a)** square, rhombus
　　(b) rectangle, square
　　(c) square, rectangle
　　(d) square, rectangle, rhombus, parallelogram
　　(e) square, rectangle
　　(f) square, rectangle, parallelogram, rhombus
　　(g) square, rhombus, kite
　　(h) rhombus, square, kite
　　(i) rhombus, square, kite

2 **(a)** $x = 69°$
　　(b) $x = 64°$
　　(c) $x = 52°$
　　(d) $x = 115°$
　　(e) $x = 30°$; $2x = 60°$; $3x = 90°$
　　(f) $a = 44°$; $b = 68°$; $c = d = 68°$; $e = 44°$

Exercise 3.4

1 **(a)** $60°$　　**(b)** $720°$　　**(c)** $120°$

2 **(a)** $1080°$　　**(b)** $1440°$　　**(c)** $2340°$

3 $\dfrac{900}{7} = 128.57°$

4 20 sides

5 **(a)** 165.6　　**(b)** $\dfrac{360}{14.4} = 25$ sides

Exercise 3.5

Diagram	Name	Definition
	circumference	distance round the outside of a circle
	diameter	distance across a circle through centre
	radius	distance from centre to circumference; half a diameter
	arc	part of the circumference of a circle
	chord	line joining any two points on the circumference
	semi-circle	half a circle
	segment	piece of circle created by chord
	sector	slice of circle; area between two radii
	tangent	line that touches a circle at one point only

Exercise 3.6

1, 2 student's own diagrams

3 2.1 cm

4 (a) scalene (b) yes

5 6.6 cm

Mixed exercise

1 (a) when two parallel lines are cut by a transversal, the alternate angles are formed inside the parallel lines, on opposite sides of the transversal

(b) a triangle with two equal sides

(c) a quadrilateral with two pairs of adjacent sides equal in length

(d) a quadrilateral with four equal sides and opposite sides parallel to each other

(e) a many-sided shape with all sides equal and all interior angles equal

(f) an eight-sided shape

2 (a) $x = 113°$

(b) $x = 41°$

(c) $x = 89°$

(d) $x = 66°$

(e) $x = 74°$; $y = 106°$; $z = 46°$

(f) $x = 38°$; $y = 104°$

(g) $x = 110°$; $y = 124°$

(h) $x = 40°$; $y = 70°$; $z = 70°$

3 (a) $x = 60 + 60 + 120 = 240°$

(b) $x = 90 + 90 + 135 = 315°$

4 (a) (i) radius (ii) chord (iii) diameter

(b) AO, DO, OC, OB

(c) 24.8 cm

(d) student's own diagram

5 student's own diagram

6 student's own diagram

Chapter 4

Exercise 4.1

1 (a) gender, eye colour, hair colour

(b) height, shoe size, mass, number of brothers/sisters

(c) shoe size, number of brothers/sisters

(d) height, mass

(e) possible answers include: gender, eye colour, hair colour – observation; height, mass – measured; shoe size, number of siblings – survey, questionnaire

Exercise 4.2

1

Mark	Tally	Frequency
1	/	1
2	//	2
3	//	2
4	LH1	5
5	LH1 ////	9
6	LH1 //	7
7	LH1 /	6
8	///	3
9	///	3
10	//	2

2 (a)

Score	1	2	3	4	5	6
Frequency	5	8	7	7	7	6

(b) The scores are fairly similar for even a low number of throws, so the dice is probably fair.

3 (a)

Score	Frequency
0–29	1
30–39	1
40–49	7
50–59	19
60–69	12
70–79	6
80–100	4

(b) 10 (c) 2 (d) 26

(e) There are very few marks at the low and high end of the scale.

4 (a)

Eye colour	Brown	Blue	Green
Male	4	0	1
Female	2	2	1

(b)

Hair colour	Brown	Black	Blonde
Male	2	2	1
Female	1	4	0

.

No. of brothers/sisters	0	1	2	3	4
Male	0	1	1	2	1
Female	2	1	1	1	0

(c) student's own sentences

Exercise 4.3

1 (a) pictogram
(b) number of students in each year group in a school
(c) 30 students
(d) half a stick figure
(e) 225
(f) Year 11; 285
(g) rounded; unlikely the year groups will all be multiples of 15

2 student's own chart

3 (a) number of boys and girls in class 10A
(b) 18   **(c)** 30
(d) the favourite sports of students in 10A, separated by gender
(e) athletics
(f) athletics
(g) 9

4 (a) student's own chart
(b) student's own chart

5 (a) cars   **(b)** 17%   **(c)** 11
(d) handcarts and bicycles

6 (a) student's own chart
(b) 6   **(c)** 50   **(d)** C

Mixed exercise

1 (a) survey or questionnaire
(b) discrete; you cannot have half a child
(c) quantitative; it can be counted
(d)

No. of children in family	0	1	2	3	4	5	6
Frequency	7	10	11	12	5	2	1

(e) student's own chart
(f) student's own chart

2 student's own pictogram

3 (a) compound bar chart
(b) It shows how many people, out of every 100, have a mobile phone and how many have a land line phone.
(c) No. The figures are percentages.
(d) Canada, USA and Denmark
(e) Germany, UK, Sweden and Italy
(f) Denmark
(g) own opinion with reason

Chapter 5
Exercise 5.1

1 (a) $\frac{1}{2}$ **(b)** $\frac{1}{3}$ **(c)** $\frac{1}{3}$
(d) $\frac{1}{4}$ **(e)** $\frac{1}{4}$ **(f)** $\frac{1}{8}$
(g) $\frac{1}{5}$ **(h)** $\frac{2}{3}$ **(i)** $\frac{3}{4}$ **(j)** $\frac{3}{8}$

2 (a) 33   **(b)** 300   **(c)** 25
(d) 65   **(e)** 168   **(f)** 55
(g) 117   **(h)** 48   **(i)** 104   **(j)** 63

Exercise 5.2

1 (a) $\frac{13}{6}$ **(b)** $\frac{25}{8}$ **(c)** $\frac{17}{11}$
(d) $\frac{93}{10}$ **(e)** $\frac{59}{5}$ **(f)** $\frac{15}{4}$
(g) $\frac{59}{4}$ **(h)** $\frac{25}{9}$ **(i)** $\frac{28}{3}$ **(j)** $\frac{-25}{9}$

2 (a) $\frac{1}{25}$ **(b)** $\frac{1}{10}$ **(c)** $\frac{2}{5}$
(d) $\frac{9}{20}$ **(e)** $\frac{16}{99}$ **(f)** $\frac{4}{11}$
(g) $\frac{30}{91}$ **(h)** $\frac{6}{25}$ **(i)** $\frac{15}{28}$ **(j)** $\frac{9}{44}$

3 (a) $\frac{108}{5}$ **(b)** $\frac{63}{13}$ **(c)** 14
(d) $\frac{28}{5}$ **(e)** 3   **(f)** $\frac{6}{19}$
(g) 120   **(h)** $\frac{3}{14}$ **(i)** 72
(j) 3   **(k)** $\frac{233}{50}$ **(l)** $\frac{7}{4}$

4 (a) $\frac{11}{20}$ **(b)** $\frac{11}{30}$ **(c)** $\frac{4}{45}$
(d) $\frac{13}{24}$ **(e)** $\frac{4}{15}$ **(f)** $\frac{19}{60}$

(g) $\frac{19}{21}$ **(h)** $\frac{16}{15}$ **(i)** $\frac{13}{24}$
(j) $\frac{35}{6}$ **(k)** $\frac{183}{56}$ **(l)** $\frac{161}{20}$
(m) $\frac{18}{65}$ **(n)** $\frac{41}{40}$ **(o)** $\frac{29}{21}$
(p) $\frac{-5}{6}$ **(q)** $\frac{-10}{3}$ **(r)** $\frac{-26}{9}$
(s) $\frac{13}{21}$ **(t)** $\frac{43}{12}$

5 (a) 24   **(b)** $\frac{96}{7}$ **(c)** $\frac{7}{96}$
(d) $\frac{10}{27}$ **(e)** $\frac{10}{9}$ **(f)** $\frac{9}{14}$

6 (a) $\frac{38}{9}$ **(b)** $\frac{4}{5}$ **(c)** $\frac{39}{7}$
(d) $\frac{19}{4}$ **(e)** $\frac{5}{12}$ **(f)** $\frac{215}{72}$
(g) 0   **(h)** $\frac{11}{170}$ **(i)** $\frac{187}{9}$

7 (a) $525   **(b)** $375

8 (a) 300
(b) 450 per day × 5 days = 2250 tiles per week

Exercise 5.3 A

1 (a) 50%   **(b)** 67%   **(c)** 16.7%
(d) 62.5%   **(e)** 29.8%   **(f)** 30%
(g) 4%   **(h)** 47%   **(i)** 112%
(j) 207%

2 (a) $\frac{1}{4}$ **(b)** $\frac{4}{5}$ **(c)** $\frac{9}{10}$
(d) $\frac{1}{8}$ **(e)** $\frac{1}{2}$ **(f)** $\frac{49}{50}$
(g) $\frac{3}{5}$ **(h)** $\frac{11}{50}$

3 (a) 60 kg   **(b)** $24
(c) 150 litres   **(d)** 55 ml
(e) $64   **(f)** £19.5
(g) 18 km   **(h)** 0.2 grams
(i) $2.08   **(j)** 47.5
(k) $2   **(l)** 4.2 kg

4 (a) +20%   **(b)** −10%
(c) +53.3%   **(d)** +3.3%
(e) −28.3%   **(f)** +33.3%
(g) +2566.7%

5 (a) $54.72   **(b)** $945
(c) $32.28   **(d)** $40 236
(e) $98.55   **(f)** $99.68

6 (a) $58.48   (b) $520
(c) $83.16   (d) $19 882
(e) $76.93   (f) $45.24

Exercise 5.3 B

1 28 595 tickets

2 1800 shares

3 $129 375

4 21.95%

5 $15 696

6 $6228

7 2.5 grams

8 $\frac{7}{25} = 28\%$ increase, so $7 more is better

Exercise 5.4 A

1 (a) 4.5×10^4 (b) 8×10^5
(c) 8×10 (d) 2.345×10^6
(e) 4.19×10^6 (f) 3.2×10^{10}
(g) 6.5×10^{-3} (h) 9×10^{-3}
(i) 4.5×10^{-4} (j) 8×10^{-7}
(k) 6.75×10^{-3} (l) 4.5×10^{-10}

2 (a) 2500   (b) 39 000
(c) 426 500   (d) 0.00001045
(e) 0.00000915   (f) 0.000000001
(g) 0.000028   (h) 94 000 000
(i) 0.00245

Exercise 5.4 B

1 (a) 5.62×10^{21}
(b) 6.56×10^{-17}
(c) 1.28×10^{-14}
(d) 1.44×10^{13}
(e) 1.58×10^{-20}
(f) 5.04×10^{18}
(g) 1.98×10^{12}
(h) 1.52×10^{17}
(i) 2.29×10^8

2 (a) 12×10^{30}
(b) 4.5×10^{11}
(c) 3.375×10^{36}
(d) 1.32×10^{-11}
(e) 2×10^{26}
(f) 2.67×10^5
(g) 1.2×10^2
(h) 2×10^{-3}
(i) 2.09×10^{-8}

3 (a) the Sun   (b) 6.051×10^6

4 (a) 500 seconds $= 5 \times 10^2$ seconds
(b) 19 166.67 seconds $= 1.92 \times 10^4$ seconds

Exercise 5.5

1 (a) $4 \times 5 = 20$
(b) $70 \times 5 = 350$
(c) $1000 \times 7 = 7000$
(d) $42 \div 6 = 7$

2 (a) 20   (b) 3
(c) 12   (d) 243

Mixed exercise

1 (a) 40   (b) 6
(c) 22   (d) 72

2 (a) $\frac{4}{5}$ (b) $\frac{2}{3}$ (c) $\frac{2}{3}$

3 (a) $\frac{1}{6}$ (b) 63   (c) $\frac{5}{3}$
(d) $\frac{13}{15}$ (e) $\frac{3}{44}$ (f) $\frac{31}{48}$
(g) $\frac{71}{6}$ (h) $\frac{361}{16}$ (i) $\frac{334}{45}$

4 $\frac{1}{4}$

5 (a) 8%   (b) 5%   (c) 63.33%

6 2.67%

7 (a) 24.6 kg   (b) 0.5l   (c) $70

8 (a) 12.5%   (b) 33.33%   (c) 34%

9 $103.50

10 $37.40

11 67.9%

12 2940 m

13 (a) $760   (b) $40 000

14 (a) 5.9×10^9 km
(b) 5.753×10^9 km

Chapter 6

Exercise 6.1

1 (a) $-2x - 2y$ (b) $-5a + 5b$
(c) $6x - 3y$ (d) $8x - 4xy$
(e) $-2x^2 - 6xy$ (f) $-9x + 9$
(g) $12 - 6a$ (h) $3 - 4x - y$
(i) 3   (j) $-3x - 7$
(k) $2x^2 - 2xy$ (l) $-3x^2 + 6xy$

2 (a) $14x - 2y - 9x$
(b) $-5xy + 10x$
(c) $6x - 6y - 2xy$
(d) $-2x - 5y - 2xy$
(e) $12xy - 14 - y + 3x$
(f) $4x^2 - 2x^2y - 3y$
(g) $-2x^2 + 2x + 5$
(h) $6x^2 + 4y - 8xy$
(i) $-\frac{1}{2}(8x - 2) + 3 - (x + 7)$

Exercise 6.2

1 (a) $x = 16$ (b) $x = 24$
(c) $x = 8$ (d) $x = 54$
(e) $x = 7$ (f) $x = -2$
(g) $x = -16$ (h) $x = -60$
(i) $x = -9$ (j) $x = -15$
(k) $x = 13$ (l) $x = 15$

2 (a) $x = 8$ (b) $x = 15$
(c) $x = -\frac{5}{2} = -2\frac{1}{2}$ (d) $x = -10$
(e) $x = -4$ (f) $x = -12$

3 (a) $x = 3$ (b) $x = 4$
(c) $x = \frac{9}{2} = 4\frac{1}{2}$ (d) $x = 4$
(e) $x = \frac{36}{10} = \frac{18}{5} = 3\frac{3}{5}$ (f) $x = 5$
(g) $x = 2$ (h) $x = -5$
(i) $x = 4$ (j) $x = -\frac{3}{2} = -1\frac{1}{2}$
(k) $x = \frac{11}{2} = 5\frac{1}{2}$ (l) $x = 3$

4 (a) $x = 10$ (b) $x = -2$
(c) $x = -\frac{8}{3} = -2\frac{2}{3}$ (d) $x = \frac{4}{3} = 1\frac{1}{3}$
(e) $x = 8$ (f) $x = \frac{1}{4}$
(g) $x = -4$ (h) $x = -9$
(i) $x = -10$ (j) $x = -13$
(k) $x = -34$ (l) $x = \frac{20}{13} = 1\frac{7}{13}$

5 (a) $x = 18$ (b) $x = 27$
(c) $x = 24$ (d) $x = -44$
(e) $x = 17$ (f) $x = 29$
(g) $x = 11$ (h) $x = \frac{23}{6} = 3\frac{5}{6}$
(i) $x = -1$ (j) $x = \frac{9}{2} = 4\frac{1}{2}$
(k) $x = -\frac{1}{3}$ (l) $x = 9$
(m) $x = \frac{16}{13} = 1\frac{3}{13}$ (n) $x = 10$
(o) $x = 42$ (p) $x = \frac{-4}{11}$

Exercise 12.3

1

Score	Frequency
0	6
1	6
2	10
3	11
4	5
5	1
6	1
Total	40

(a) 2.25 (b) 3 (c) 2
(d) 6

2

Data set	A	B	C
mean	3.5	46.14	4.12
median	3	40	4.5
mode	3 and 5	40	6.5

Mixed exercise

1 (a) mean 6.4, median 6, mode 6, range 6
 (b) mean 2.6, median 2, mode 2, range 5
 (c) mean 13.8, median 12.8, no mode, range 11.9

2 (a) 19 (b) 9 and 10 (c) 5.66

3 C – although B's mean is bigger it has a larger range. C's smaller range suggests that its mean is probably more representative.

4 (a) 4.82 cm³ (b) 5 cm³
 (c) 5 cm³

Chapter 13
Exercise 13.1

1 student's own diagrams

2 (a) 2600 m (b) 230 mm
 (c) 820 cm (d) 2450.809 km
 (e) 20 mm (f) 0.157 m

3 (a) 9080 g (b) 49 340 g
 (c) 500 g (d) 0.068 kg
 (e) 0.0152 kg (f) 2.3 tonne

4 (a) 19 km 100 m
 (b) 9015 cm 15 cm
 (c) 435 mm 2 mm
 (d) 492 cm 63 cm
 (e) 635 m 35 m
 (f) 580 500 cm 500 cm

5 (a) 1200 mm² (b) 900 mm²
 (c) 16 420 mm² (d) 370 000 m²
 (e) 0.009441 km² (f) 423 000 mm²

6 (a) 69 000 mm³
 (b) 19 000 mm³
 (c) 30 040 mm³
 (d) 4 815 000 cm³
 (e) 0.103 cm³
 (f) 0.0000469 m³

7 220 m

8 110 cm

9 42 cm

10 88 (round down as you cannot have part of a box)

Exercise 13.2

1

Name	Time in	Time out	Lunch	(a) Hours worked	(b) Daily earnings
Dawoot	$\frac{1}{4}$ past 9	Half past five	$\frac{3}{4}$ hour	$7\frac{1}{2}$ hours	$55.88
Nadira	8:17 a.m.	5:30 p.m.	$\frac{1}{2}$ hour	8 h 43 min	$64.94
John	08:23	17:50	45 min	8 h 42 min	$64.82
Robyn	7:22 a.m.	4:30 p.m.	1 hour	8 h 8 min	$60.59
Mari	08:08	18:30	45 min	9 h 37 min	$71.64

2 6 h 25 min

3 20 min

4 (a) 5 h 47 min (b) 11 h 26 min
 (c) 12 h 12 min (d) 14 h 30 min

5 (a) 09:00 (b) 1 hour (c) 09:30
 (d) 30 minutes
 (e) It would arrive late at Peron Place at 10:54 and at Marquez Lane at 11:19.

Exercise 13.3

1 The upper bound is 'inexact' so 42.5 in table means < 42.5

	Upper bound	Lower bound
(a)	42.5	41.5
(b)	13325.5	13324.5
(c)	450	350
(d)	12.245	12.235
(e)	11.495	11.485
(f)	2.55	2.45
(g)	395	385
(h)	1.1325	1.1315

2 (a) $71.5 \leq h < 72.5$
 (b) Yes, it is less than 72.5 (although it would be impossible to measure to that accuracy).

Exercise 13.4

1 (a) 1 unit = 100 000 rupiah
 (b) (i) 250 000
  (ii) 500 000
  (iii) 2 500 000
 (c) (i) Aus$80
  (ii) Aus$640

2 (a) Temperature in degrees C against temperature in degrees F
 (b) (i) 32 °F (ii) 50 °F
  (iii) 220 °F
 (c) oven could be marked in Fahrenheit, but of course she could also have experienced a power failure or other practical problem
 (d) Fahrenheit scale as 50 °C is hot, not cold

3 (a) 9 kg (b) 45 kg
 (c) (i) 20 kg (ii) 35 kg
  (iii) 145 lb

Exercise 13.5

1 (a) (i) US$1 = ¥76.16
  (ii) £1 = NZ$1.99
  (iii) €1 = IR69.10
  (iv) Can$1 = €0.71
  (v) ¥1 = £0.01
  (vi) R1 = US$0.12

(b) (i) 2490.50   **(ii)** 41 460
   (iii) 7540.15
(c) (i) 9139.20   **(ii)** 52 820
   (iii) 145 632

Mixed exercise

1 (a) 2700 m   **(b)** 690 mm
   (c) 6000 kg   **(d)** 0.0235 kg
   (e) 263 000 mg   **(f)** 29 250 ml
   (g) 0.24 l   **(h)** 1000 mm²
   (i) 0.006428 km² **(j)** 7 900 000 cm³
   (k) 29 000 000 m³ **(l)** 0.168 cm³

2 23 min 45 s

3 2 h 19 min 55 s

4 $1.615\,\text{m} \le h < 1.625\,\text{m}$

5 (a) No, that is lower than the lower
   bound of 45
   (b) Yes, that is within the bounds

6 (a) conversion graph showing litres
   against gallons (conversion factor)
   (b) (i) 45 l   **(ii)** 112.5 l
   (c) (i) 3.33 gallons **(ii)** 26.67 gallons
   (d) (i) 48.3 km/g and 67.62 km/g
      (ii) 10.62 km/l and 14.87 km/l

7 €892.06

8 (a) US$1 = IR49.81   **(b)** 99 620
   (c) US$249.95

9 £4239.13

Chapter 14

Exercise 14.1

1 (a)

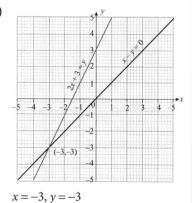

$x = -3, y = -3$

(b)

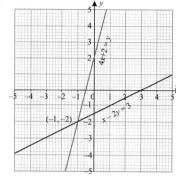

$x = -1, y = -2$

(c)

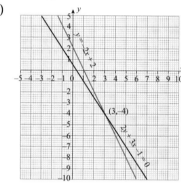

$x = 3, y = -4$

(d)

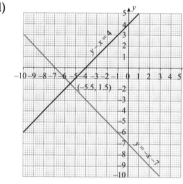

$x = -5.5, y = -1.5$

(e)

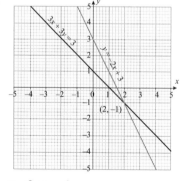

$x = 2, y = -1$

2 (a) (i) $y = -x + 4$
     (ii) $2y = 3x + 12$

     (iii) $y = -4x - 2$
     (iv) $y = x$
     (v) $y = -2$
     (vi) $y = x - 4$
 (b) (i) $(-2, 6)$ **(ii)** $(-2, -2)$
     (iii) $(4, 0)$

3 (a) $x = 4, y = 2$
   (b) $x = -1, y = 2$
   (c) $x = 0, y = 4$
   (d) $x = 3, y = 1$

4 (a) $x = 6, y = -1$
   (b) $x = 1, y = 2$
   (c) $x = 18, y = -8$
   (d) $x = 1, y = 1\frac{1}{3}$
   (e) $x = 3, y = -1$
   (f) $x = 3, y = 7$

5 (a) $x = 2, y = 1$
   (b) $x = 2, y = 2$
   (c) $x = 2, y = -1$
   (d) $x = 3, y = 2$
   (e) $x = 3, y = 2.5$
   (f) $x = 4, y = 2$
   (g) $x = 5, y = 3$
   (h) $x = 0.5, y = -0.5$
   (i) $x = -9, y = -2$

6 a chocolate bar costs $1.20 and a box
  of gums $0.75

7 number of students is 7

8 6 quarters and 6 dimes

Mixed exercise

1 $x = 2 \; y = -5$

2 $x = -2 \; y = 5$

3 $5000 at 5% and $10 000 at 8%

4 Solve $5L - 2B = 12$ and $2L + 2B = 9$
  simultaneously.
  $L = 3$ metres and $B = 1.5$ metres

5 (a) $2x + 5y = 30$ and $x - 5y = 10$
   (b) $x = 13\frac{1}{3}$ and $y = \frac{2}{3}$
   (c) $2x + 5y = 30$
       $x - 5y = 10$
         $3x = 40$
          $x = 13.33...$
          $y = 0.66...$

Chapter 15

Exercise 15.1

1 (a) length = 10 cm, width = 7 cm
   (b) length = 14.4 cm, width = 7 cm

2 (a) length = 9.14 cm, width = 5.5 cm
   (b) Yes. The length of the mini pitch = width of standard pitch and 2 × width of mini pitch < length of standard pitch. It is possible to have two mini pitches on a standard pitch so, with three standard pitches, up to six matches could take place at the same time.

3 (a) $\frac{1}{200}$ or $\frac{1}{150}$
   (b) (i) and (ii) diagram drawn using student's scale including x for net posts

4 (a) student's scale drawing – diagonal distance = 11.3 m
   (b) using Pythagoras' theorem

Exercise 15.2

1 (a) 090°
   (b) 225°
   (c) 315°

2 (a) 250° (b) 310°
   (c) 135°

3 student's drawing
   (a) 223° (b) 065° (c) 11 km
   (d) 13 km

Exercise 15.3

1

	(a)	(b)	(c)	(d)
hypotenuse	c	z	f	q
opp(A)	a	y	g	p
adj(A)	b	x	e	r

2 (a) opp(30°) = x cm
      adj(60°) = x cm
      opp(60°) = adj(30°) = y cm
   (b) adj(40°) = q cm
      opp(50°) = q cm
      opp(40°) = adj(50°) = p cm

3 (a) 0.65 (b) 1.43 (c) 5.14
   (d) 0.41 (e) 0

---

4 (a) $\tan A = \frac{3}{4}$ (b) $\tan x = \frac{2}{3}$, $\tan y = \frac{3}{2}$
   (c) $\tan 55° = \frac{1}{d}$, $\tan B = d$
   (d) $\tan y = \frac{5}{12}$, $\angle X = (90 - y)°$, $\tan X = \frac{12}{5}$
   (e) $AC = 2$ cm, $\tan B = \frac{4}{3}$, $\tan C = \frac{3}{4}$

5 (a) $x = 1.40$ cm
   (b) $y = 19.29$ m
   (c) $c = 3.32$ cm
   (d) $a = 13$ m
   (e) $x = 35.70$ cm

6 (a) 26.6° (b) 40.9° (c) 51.3°
   (d) 85.2° (e) 14.0° (f) 40.9°
   (g) 79.7° (h) 44.1°

7 (a) 16° (b) 46° (c) 49°
   (d) 23° (e) 38°

8 (a) hyp = y, adj(θ) = z, $\cos\theta = \frac{z}{y}$
   (b) hyp = c, adj(θ) = b, $\cos\theta = \frac{b}{c}$
   (c) hyp = c, adj(θ) = a, $\cos\theta = \frac{a}{c}$
   (d) hyp = p, adj(θ) = r, $\cos\theta = \frac{r}{p}$
   (e) hyp = x, adj(θ) = z, $\cos\theta = \frac{z}{x}$

9 (a) $\sin A = \frac{7}{13}$, $\cos A = \frac{12}{13}$, $\tan A = \frac{7}{12}$
   (b) $\sin B = \frac{5}{11}$, $\cos B = \frac{19.6}{22}$, $\tan B = \frac{10}{19.6}$
   (c) $\sin C = \frac{3}{5}$, $\cos C = \frac{4}{5}$, $\tan C = \frac{3}{4}$
   (d) $\sin D = \frac{63}{65}$, $\cos D = \frac{16}{65}$, $\tan D = \frac{63}{16}$
   (e) $\sin E = \frac{84}{85}$, $\cos E = \frac{13}{85}$, $\tan E = \frac{84}{13}$

10 (a) 45° (b) 64° (c) 57°
   (d) 60° (e) 30° (f) 27°

11 4.86 m

Mixed exercise

1. (a) $x = 37.6°$ (b) $x = 44.0°$

2 53.5°, 90°

Chapter 16

1 (a) E (b) C (c) A
   (d) D (e) B

---

2 (a) student's own line (line should go close to (160, 4.5) and (170, 5.5)) answers (b) and (c) depend on student's best fit line
   (b) ≈ 4.75 m
   (c) between 175 and 180 cm
   (d) fairly strongly positive
   (e) taller athletes can jump further

Mixed exercise

1 (a) the number of accidents for different speeds
   (b) average speed
      answers to (c) depend on student's best fit line
   (c) (i) ≈ 35 accidents
      (ii) < 40 km/h
   (d) strong positive
   (e) there are more accidents when vehicles are travelling at a higher average speed

2 (a) there a strong negative correlation at first, but this becomes weaker as the cars get older
   (b) 0–2 years
   (c) it stabilises around the $6000 level
   (d) 2–3 years
   (e) 5–8 thousand dollars

Chapter 17

Exercise 17.1

1 $19.26

2 $25 560

3 (a) €930.75 (b) €1083.75
   (c) €765 (d) €1179.38

4 $1203.40

5 $542.75

6 (a) $625 (b) $25 (c) $506.50

Exercise 17.2

1 (a) $7.50 (b) $160 (c) $210
   (d) $448 (e) $343.75

2 5 years

3 2.8%

4 $2800 more

5 $2281 more

6 (a) $7.50 (b) $187.73

(c) $225.75 **(d)** $574.55
(e) $346.08

7 $562.75

8 $27 085.85

Exercise 17.3

1 **(a)** $100 **(b)** $200 **(c)** $340
(d) $900

2 $300

3 $500

4 $64.41

5 **(a)** $179.10
(b) $40.04
(c) $963.90

Mixed exercise

1 **(a)** 12 h **(b)** 40 h **(c)** $25\frac{1}{2}$ h

2 **(a)** $1190 **(b)** $1386 **(c)** $1232

3 **(a)** $62 808 **(b)** $4149.02

4 **(a)**

Years	Simple interest	Compound interest
1	300	300
2	600	609
3	900	927.27
4	1200	1125.09
5	1500	1592.74
6	1800	1940.52
7	2100	2298.74
8	2400	2667.70

(b) $92.74
(c) student's own graph; a comment such as, the amount of compound interest increases faster than the simple interest

5 $862.50

6 $3360

7 **(a)** $1335, $2225
(b) $1950, $3250
(c) $18 000, $30 000

8 **(a)** $4818 **(b)** 120%

9 $425

10 $211.20

11 $43.36 (each)

12 $204

Chapter 18

Exercise 18.1

1

x	–3	–2	–1	0	1	2	3
(a) $y = -x^2 + 2$	–7	–2	1	2	1	–2	–7
(b) $y = x^2 - 3$	6	1	–2	–3	–2	1	6
(c) $y = -x^2 - 2$	–11	–6	–3	–2	–3	–6	–11
(d) $y = -x^2 - 3$	–12	–7	–4	–3	–4	–7	–12
(e) $y = x^2 + \frac{1}{2}$	9.5	4.5	1.5	0.5	1.5	4.5	9.5

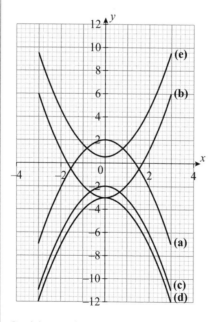

2 **(a)** $y = x^2 + 3$ **(b)** $y = x^2 + 2$
(c) $y = x^2$ **(d)** $y = -x^2 + 3$
(e) $y = -x^2 - 4$

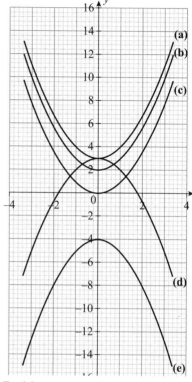

3 **(a)**

x	–2	–1	0	1	2	3	4	5
$y = x^2 - 3x + 2$	12	6	2	0	0	2	6	12

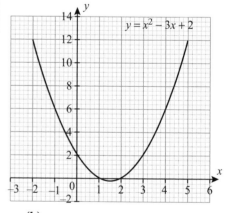

(b)

x	–3	–2	–1	0	1	2	3
$y = x^2 - 2x - 1$	14	7	2	–1	–2	–1	2

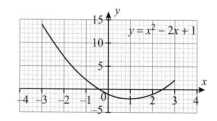